Palgrave Studies in Institutions, Economics and Law

Series Editors
Alain Marciano
University of Montpellier
Montpellier, France

Giovanni Ramello
University of Eastern Piedmont
Alessandria, Italy

Law and Economics is an interdisciplinary field of research that has emerged in recent decades, with research output increasing dramatically and academic programmes in law and economics multiplying. Increasingly, legal cases have an economic dimension and economic matters depend on rules and regulations. Increasingly, economists have realized that "institutions matter" because they influence economic activities. Increasingly, too, economics is used to improve our understanding of how institutions and how legal systems work. This new Palgrave Pivot series studies the intersection between law and economics, and addresses the need for greater interaction between the two disciplines.

More information about this series at
http://www.palgrave.com/gp/series/15241

Péter Cserne • Fabrizio Esposito
Editors

Economics in Legal Reasoning

palgrave
macmillan

Editors
Péter Cserne
University of Aberdeen
Aberdeen, UK

Fabrizio Esposito
Université catholique de Louvain
Louvain-la-Neuve
Belgium

ISSN 2662-6535 ISSN 2662-6543 (electronic)
Palgrave Studies in Institutions, Economics and Law
ISBN 978-3-030-40167-2 ISBN 978-3-030-40168-9 (eBook)
https://doi.org/10.1007/978-3-030-40168-9

This Palgrave Macmillan imprint is published by the registered company Springer Nature Switzerland AG.
The registered company address is: Gewerbestrasse 11, 6330 Cham, Switzerland

CONTENTS

LIST OF CONTRIBUTORS

Jan Broulík University of Amsterdam, Amsterdam, The Netherlands

Damiano Canale Università commerciale Luigi Bocconi, Milan, Italy

Péter Cserne University of Aberdeen, Aberdeen, UK

Fabrizio Esposito Université catholique de Louvain, Louvain-la-Neuve, Belgium

Felipe Figueroa Zimmermann University of Warwick, Coventry, UK

Nicola Giocoli University of Pisa, Pisa, Italy

Fernando Gómez Pomar Universitat Pompeu Fabra, Barcelona, Spain

Pavlína Hubková Université du Luxembourg, Luxembourg, Luxemburg

Giovanni Tuzet Università commerciale Luigi Bocconi, Milan, Italy

CHAPTER 1

Introduction

Péter Cserne and Fabrizio Esposito

Abstract The Introduction puts the contents of the book into perspective, summarizes its aims, and gives an overview of the argument. The relative neglect of the topic of economics in legal, especially judicial, reasoning stems from the opposition of two argumentative styles in modern economics and in ordinary adjudication. Despite their differences, the commonalities between legal and economic reasoning constitute the stepping stone for investigating the role of economics in legal reasoning.

Keywords Law and economics • Economics of legal reasoning • Economics in legal reasoning • Economic view • Legal view

This book offers a concise yet comprehensive overview of the roles that economic insights play and could play in legal reasoning. Traditionally, economists have been first and foremost interested in the economic effects

P. Cserne (✉)
University of Aberdeen, Aberdeen, UK
e-mail: peter.cserne@abdn.ac.uk

F. Esposito
Université catholique de Louvain, Louvain-la-Neuve, Belgium
e-mail: fabrizio.esposito@uclouvain.be

© The Author(s) 2020
P. Cserne, F. Esposito (eds.), *Economics in Legal Reasoning*,
Palgrave Studies in Institutions, Economics and Law,
https://doi.org/10.1007/978-3-030-40168-9_1

1

of judicial decisions and the legal process. This line of inquiry has generated a wide-ranging literature, covering research questions, such as whether the presence of specialized courts affects the frequency of bankruptcy petitions (Detotto et al. 2019); the effect of court fees on the behavior of prospective litigants (Mora-Sanguinetti and Martínez-Matute 2019); or the role that judicial efficiency plays in reducing endogenous uncertainty in markets (Ramello et al. 2015). In addition to this literature, the interpretation of constitutions, statutes, precedents, and contracts has been the object of economic analysis (see, for example, the selection in Bix 2018).

But what if judges are not the objects but the agents of economic analysis? While there has been occasional judicial reflection on the role of "economists on the bench" (Culp 1987; Clark and Kozinski 2019), this is the first book-length study looking at the role played by economics *in* legal reasoning. Such a systematic study has a twofold goal. First, it contributes to the jurisprudential self-consciousness of Law and Economics scholars, thereby improving the chances of economic arguments having an impact on important legal decisions. As Richard Craswell argued, economists should avoid "the jurisprudential naïveté about the ultimate connection, if any, between the (…) technical economic analysis and the sorts of argument that might be acceptable to courts" (Craswell 1993, p. 293).

Second, it suggests a step change in how economics contributes to public discourse about adjudication. Theoretical and empirical findings on judicial decision-making bear relevance for (small-scale, marginal) legal reforms and (large-scale, total) institutional design. Both may be complex as the difficulties of competent decision-making arise within complex legal systems, and these systems already use various mechanisms to mitigate problems of legitimacy and expertise. Therefore, the difficulties of competent adjudication are partly generated by the very institutional setting of adjudication.

Hence, to be heard by judicial insiders, economists need to pay closer attention to the insider perspective of legal practice.

By offering an overview of the relationship between economics and legal reasoning, this book shows economists that a more thorough study of legal reasoning is worth the effort. The topic should also be of interest to the legal community, where both supporters and critics of Law and Economics will be exposed to a yet-to-be developed area of interaction between the disciplines, to the effect that the book has the potential of spurring a wider debate.

At the outset, it is worth looking at the reasons for the relative neglect of this topic. We suggest that these are related to two different argumentative styles. In the Law and Economics literature, the difference has been usually epitomized as the opposition between *ex post* legal reasoning and *ex ante* economic reasoning (Easterbrook 1984). Indeed, traditionally, legal, and especially judicial, reasoning has been backward-looking: it is in preexisting norms that the authority of adjudication is based and reasoning is about justifying a decision about facts that happened in the past. There is a rich tradition and lively academic literature that aims at understanding legal reasoning in hermeneutical, logical, or rhetorical terms. Chapter 2 by Canale and Tuzet offers a clear and concise introduction to legal reasoning from a legal point of view. Implicit in this literature is the assumption that legal practice is relatively autonomous and sets its own conventional (jurisdiction-specific, relatively flexible, and evolving) criteria for acceptable arguments.

In its modern self-understanding, economics is scientific and objective, and focuses on investigating the causes and effects of (economic) behavior. To this end, economists have been developing a wide set of techniques and methods. It is therefore quite natural for the economic analysis of law to approach legal phenomena relying primarily on those techniques and methods, thereby formulating propositions about causes and effects of laws. For economists, the law is not merely a mechanism of peaceful conflict resolution: they are primarily interested in legal processes because the manner in which disputes are resolved in the (shadow of the) legal system has important effects on the level of transaction costs, on the possibility of moral hazard and opportunistic behavior, on the incentives to innovate, and so on; thus, by studying the economic effects of the law, economists can help improve the functioning of the legal system.

Economists generally focus on the outcome of legal cases or, less frequently, on the motivational determinants and institutional context of judicial behavior; legal processes and doctrines only matter insofar as they have an impact on the incentives of agents or the costs of legal processes. The disregard for legal process and doctrine is related to the underlying assumptions of economic models focusing on instrumental rationality and aggregative measures of welfare. It is also motivated by economists' political or moral "realism", similar to Bentham's project of demystifying the law, and in its zeal reminiscent of Bentham's impatience with common law and the legal profession (Postema 2019).

From a jurisprudential perspective, the economic view of law may seem overly reductive and superficial. Even if the role of economic expertise in legislation and in specific legal processes is generally acknowledged, economics is often perceived as alien to judicial reasoning. This external perspective is clearly different from the one legal scholars are used to. Could economics, then, as an explanatory social science contribute not only to policy debates but also provide an input to adjudication directly? Indeed, there is ample room for economic analysis within the parameters of legal objectives. As Cserne argues in Chap. 3, economics can either provide arguments within the parameters of legal discourse (economics in legal reasoning) or retain an external perspective (economics of legal reasoning).

As Chap. 4 by Hubková demonstrates, judicial reasoning is commonly confronted with concepts, arguments, and theories that are economic in character, and judicial activity involves economic considerations more generally: these stand to benefit from more self-consciousness. Her typology of the ways in which economics customarily informs legal reasoning suggests that the old adage *iudex non calculat* is not really true. Having said that, the institutional features of legal decision-making, especially those relating to the availability of data, resources, and training of judges, determine the role of economic inputs in legal discourse.

In a subtler way, the normative concerns and institutional constraints of adjudication come together to form a dominant judicial mindset, which is reproduced and reinforced by education and professional socialization. Gómez Pomar discusses these issues in Chap. 5, noting that even in explicitly economic areas of the law such as market regulation, the decisions of the European Court of Justice illustrate how legal reasoning may focus on a narrow set of considerations and ignore empirical information and forward-looking considerations suggested by economics, thereby missing the bigger picture.

In the most general sense, the judicial reluctance to embrace economic considerations is linked to the competence of courts—to the functional constraints under which adjudication is exercised. 'Competence' is a multi-faced, technical, institutional, and normative feature of adjudication. It has at least two aspects: legitimacy and expertise. The first relates to judicial authority, accountability, and discretion; the second to epistemic and institutional features of judicial decision-making. A key issue in terms of both legitimacy and expertise is "the tension between providing a satisfactory outcome ex post to the parties in the individual dispute (...) and issuing a statement of principle to influence ex ante the behavior of other individuals and groups" (Ogus 2006, p. 303). To be sure, even the *ex post* perspective does not rule out economic inputs. Yet when judges embrace purposive or teleological reasoning, this can be modeled as at least incomplete or partial economic reasoning: a rational choice among means in light of expected consequences.

Two further chapters analyze how economics may enter legal reasoning through the establishment of facts and the specification of technical norms. Chapter 6 by Broulík demonstrates that in specific contexts such as the calculation of lost earnings in personal injury cases or the identification and measurement of the anticompetitive effects of business conduct, adjudication has been relying on sophisticated economic input ("forensic economics") for decades. Indeed, as the case study by Giocoli in Chap. 7 illustrates, the US federal legal system has developed detailed procedural rules to channel the clash between sophisticated economic and legal expertise in antitrust cases—and this oblique regulation of the market for economic expertise through rules of evidence produces perplexing results. The general message is that economists overlook legal doctrine and reasoning at their own risk and peril.

The apparent clash between the argumentative styles of economics and law may easily result in mutual misrepresentation, misunderstanding, and mistrust. From the perspective of the classical tradition of rhetoric and practical reasoning, the contrast between the way modern economics tends to argue, deductive logic and statistical generalization, and legal reasoning, which is about the practice of persuasion, is more apparent than real (McCloskey 1988). Both economics and law are disciplines of systematic reflection on practical matters, displaying aspects of the same practical rationality (Cserne 2019). The last two chapters, however, provide two novel ways to overcome these disciplinary conflicts.

In Chap. 8, Figueroa-Zimmerman focuses on the relative epistemic authority of the two disciplines. He identifies a dynamic where reductionist explanations of legal phenomena by economists are countered by legal scholars pointing out features of legal practice that are irreducible expressions of normative commitments. He suggests overcoming this dynamic through increased reflexivity and a version of legal realism which can successfully restore the epistemic balance of the disciplines.

Last but not least, Chap. 9 by Esposito shows that it is possible to search for economic concepts in legal rules and doctrine systematically. He suggests that legal reasoning can be "reverse engineered", once the argumentative implications of different economic concepts are made explicit and tested against the content of actual legal reasoning.

Once one approaches the relationship between economics and legal reasoning with a curious and charitable mindset, it becomes clear that despite their differences, economics and legal reasoning interact in many subtle and unexpected ways. This book offers a fast track to access and appreciate these interactions. Hopefully, this book will inspire further systematic, sophisticated thinking about adjudication and its reforms, combining insights from legal scholarship and economics in an intelligent and effective way.

REFERENCES

Bix, Brian, ed. 2018. *Economic Approaches to Legal Reasoning and Interpretation*. Cheltenham: Edward Elgar.

Clark, Conor, and Alex Kozinski. 2019. Does Law and Economics Help Decide Cases? *European Journal of Law and Economics* 48: 89–111.

Craswell, Richard. 1993. Default Rules, Efficiency, and Prudence. *Southern California Interdisciplinary Law Journal* 3: 289–302.

Cserne, Péter. 2019. Knowledge Claims in Law and Economics: Gaps and Bridges between Theoretical and Practical Rationality. In *Law and Economics as Interdisciplinary Exchange: Philosophical, Methodological and Historical Perspectives*, ed. Péter Cserne and Magdalena Małecka, 9–30. Abingdon, Oxon and New York: Routledge.

Culp, Jerome M., ed. 1987. Symposium: Economists on the Bench. *Law and Contemporary Problems* 50 (4). https://scholarship.law.duke.edu/lcp/vol50/iss4/

Detotto, Claudio, Laura Serra, and Marco Vannini. 2019. Did Specialised Courts Affect the Frequency of Business Bankruptcy Petitions in Spain? *European Journal of Law and Economics* 47: 125–145.

Easterbrook, Frank H. 1984. Foreword: The Court and the Economic System. *Harvard Law Review* 98: 4–60.

McCloskey, Donald M. 1988. The Rhetoric of Law and Economics. *Michigan Law Review* 86: 752–767.

Mora-Sanguinetti, Juan S., and Marta Martínez-Matute. 2019. An Economic Analysis of Court Fees: Evidence from the Spanish Civil Jurisdiction. *European Journal of Law and Economics* 47: 321–359.

Ogus, Anthony. 2006. *Costs and Cautionary Tales: Economic Insights for the Law*. Oxford: Hart.

Postema, Gerald J. 2019. *Bentham and the Common Law Tradition*. 2nd ed. New York: Oxford University Press.

Ramello, Giovanni Battista, Roberto Ippoliti, and Alessandro Melcarne. 2015. Judicial Efficiency and Entrepreneurs' Expectations on the Reliability of European Legal Systems. *European Journal of Law and Economics* 40: 75–94.

PART I

Foundations

CHAPTER 2

What Is Legal Reasoning About: A Jurisprudential Account

Damiano Canale and Giovanni Tuzet

Abstract Legal reasoning is about the creation, application, and extinction of legal norms (rules, standards, or principles). Legislators and lawmakers argue about the creation and extinction of norms, or, more technically, about the enactment and abrogation of norms by the competent legal authorities. Judges and other officials argue about the application of norms, on the basis of the interpretation of the relevant legal texts.

In the judicial context, in particular, participants make arguments about the relevant facts and the application of law to these facts. Legal arguments divide into evidentiary and interpretive ones, where the former point at the reconstruction of what happened and the latter point at the ways in which legal texts can be interpreted. Both are necessary in the application of law.

Keywords Legal reasoning • Interpretive argument • Evidentiary argument • Fact • Norm

D. Canale • G. Tuzet (✉)
Università commerciale Luigi Bocconi, Milan, Italy
e-mail: damiano.canale@unibocconi.it; giovanni.tuzet@unibocconi.it

© The Author(s) 2020   9
P. Cserne, F. Esposito (eds.), *Economics in Legal Reasoning*,
Palgrave Studies in Institutions, Economics and Law,
https://doi.org/10.1007/978-3-030-40168-9_2

2.1   LEGAL REASONING AS CONTEXTUAL

Legal reasoning is about the creation, interpretation, application, and extinction of legal norms (rules, standards, or principles). Legislators and lawmakers argue about the creation and extinction of norms, or, more technically, about the enactment and abrogation of norms by the competent legal authorities. Judges and other officials mainly argue about the application of norms, on the basis of the evidence about the relevant facts and the interpretation of the relevant legal texts.

When the lawmaking process is legislative, participants give and ask for reasons in the parliamentary debates concerning a bill, and, more generally, in the political or scholarly debates about it. In these contexts, legal reasons frequently blend with political, economic, and moral reasons in favor of or against a bill.

When the process is judicial, reasons are given and asked for by the parties litigating before a judge or court. If this process has a lawmaking component, legal reasons will concern the merits or demerits of the new law; if it is basically on the interpretation and application of preexisting law, legal reasons will be about the correctness of certain ways of interpreting and applying it.

In some jurisdictions judges have lawmaking powers; in others they must restrain themselves and apply preexisting law, once the relevant texts have been considered and interpreted. And in most jurisdictions judges are supposed to justify their decisions. If their task is to correctly interpret and apply the law, they are supposed to provide the reasons that justify their decisions in those respects. Such reasons are usually given in written form, in official documents where judges indicate how they decided and why. Written judicial opinions articulate the reasons in favor of or against a certain decision.

Those reasons can be reconstructed as premises of reasoning schemes or patterns. In judicial contexts litigating parties provide them in the first place; then judges either accept or reject them insofar as their task is to assess the correctness of the interpretive and applicative claims of the parties; judges can also advance additional reasons when their decision-making powers go beyond the claims of the parties. Being advanced in public, in oral or written form, the reasoning of both parties and judges is a typical form of *argument*, properly speaking, that is the public presentation of reasons in favor of or against a litigated claim, according to logical schemes or reasoning patterns that are acceptable in the relevant context.

In the usage we adopt here, argument is wider than reasoning, and reasoning is a basic notion in that there is no argument without reasoning, while there is reasoning without argument. Some distinguishing features of an argument are that it is performed in public, that it is about a disputed point or claim, and that it is part of a dialectical exchange, where critical questions are posed and the claim is unsettled. As one scholar has put it (Walton 2018, p. 68), in an argument "the conclusion is always the claim made by one party that is doubted or is open to doubt by the other party. ... Indeed, that is the whole point of using an argument. If there is no doubt about a proposition, and everybody accepts it as true, there is no reason for arguing either for or against it."[1]

Since legal reasoning in legislative contexts is usually characterized by the presentation of reasons that are not only legal (being also political, economic, or moral),[2] the most typical forms of legal reasoning occur in judicial contexts, where claims and arguments usually have a more technical outlook. This is not to deny that extralegal considerations can play a significant role in judicial decision-making; on the contrary, this is often the case. However, from the point of view of legal justification, judicial decisions must be supported by legal reasons. Economic arguments, for instance, need to be legally relevant in order to be acceptable: they must articulate reasons that are legally relevant since a legal norm takes them into explicit consideration or because they resonate with some principle or value promoted by the legal system. Welfarist arguments, in particular, can be relevant to legislative or judicial decision-making only insofar as the pursuit of welfare is considered a legal reason within the legal system. To put it differently, one thing is the law as it is (like it or not); another is the law as it ought to be, or as we wish it to be. (Economists can think of the parallel distinction between positive and normative economic analysis).

For the reasons mentioned this chapter focuses on legal reasoning as performed in judicial contexts. In a typical dispute two parties confront each other before a third one. The litigants advance claims and counterclaims, and support them with arguments and counterarguments. If the plaintiff in a civil lawsuit states that she/he was wrongfully harmed by the defendant, then she/he has to provide reasons and arguments to that

---

[1] However, there are some uses of "arguing" that refer to solitary meditation and decision-making. Daniel Defoe represents Robison Crusoe as "arguing with himself" about what to do with the savages (e.g. Chaps. XII and XIV of Crusoe's novel).
[2] See, for example, Wintgens and Oliver-Lalana (2013).

effect. She/he must prove that she/he was harmed by the defendant and must explain why the harm was wrongful. Then the defendant can defend herself/himself by claiming, for instance, that there was no harm at all, or that the evidence presented to prove it is insufficient, or that the harm was caused by someone else, or that she/he had an excuse, or that the harm was not wrongful at all. If the plaintiff contends that she/he had an economic loss because of the defendant's activity, the defendant can try to show that such loss didn't occur, or that it is not proven, or that it was due to someone else's activity, or that she/he caused it in order to prevent a greater harm, or that the loss was not wrongful since it was the result of a fair economic competition.

Once the arguments and counterarguments are on the table, it is the third party's task to adjudicate the dispute. It can be an individual judge, or a court, or a jury. The decision-maker is supposed to evaluate the arguments and counterarguments presented and make a legal decision. If it is found that the plaintiff was wrongfully harmed, a decision must be made in her/his favor entitling her/him to some remedy like compensation. If instead the decision-maker finds for the defendant, no remedy will be given. A jury is not supposed to articulate the reasons why the case is decided in a given way. But judges and courts are supposed to do so in most contemporary legal systems. Judicial opinions, or reasoned decisions typically given in written form, articulate the reasoning whose ultimate conclusion is the outcome of the case.

Schematically, argumentative practice in judicial contexts encompasses *evidentiary* arguments that reconstruct the relevant facts of a case; *interpretive* arguments that extract legal rules, standards, or principles from authoritative texts; and *integrative* arguments that fill in the gaps in the law. At trial, the litigators support their factual and normative claims with arguments of these sorts. Evidentiary arguments are presented to support a certain version of the facts; interpretive arguments support the normative claims that a party advances given the alleged facts and the relevant authoritative texts or sources; and integrative arguments fill in the normative gaps that a legal system may present. So, legal reasoning is about these various things, namely the facts, the interpretation of texts, the filling of gaps, and the application of norms to the relevant facts.

In the following we explore some varieties of legal reasoning (Sect. 2.2) and, starting from the traditional model of the judicial syllogism, we present what we call the "double justification model" of judicial decision-making

(Sect. 2.3). This means that we will address first some *contents* of legal reasoning and then its *structure* according to the syllogistic model and the double justification model.

2.2   THE VARIETIES OF LEGAL REASONING

We won't discuss here whether legal reasoning can be formalized or rather remains an informal practice. Artificial intelligence scholars and deontic logicians provide tools and models for the purpose of formalization. Other scholars stress the dialectical and rhetorical dimensions of legal reasoning.[3] For sure, as mentioned earlier, legal reasoning is publicly performed as an argumentative effort to persuade some audience or justify a decision. Parties primarily use it to persuade judges. Judges primarily use it to justify their decisions. Let us expand on what this is about.

In the first place, in judicial contexts, legal reasoning is about the *facts* of a case (see, for example, Twining 1990; Anderson et al. 2005; Haack 2014). Evidence is collected and presented to the fact-finders. But evidence by itself is not sufficient, since parties have to construct arguments out of it. It is not sufficient, for instance, that a piece of evidence like a document or a material object be shown to the fact-finders, or that a witness be brought to the witness stand. One has to articulate what the piece of evidence is supposed to prove and how it proves it, or why the witness' testimony is credible, or why it resists the critical questions that are posed about it, and so on. The arguments used in the process of fact-finding and evidence-based inference are numerous and have varying degrees of persuasive force and justificatory power. Some traditional ones like the argument from lay testimony and the argument from documentary evidence are currently losing some of their importance whereas the arguments from scientific evidence and expert opinion are becoming more and more prominent. It is possible to provide a deductive model of reasoning on facts (Comanducci 2000), but evidentiary arguments rather exemplify nondeductive models of reasoning such as induction (Ferrer 2007), abduction (Tuzet 2003), and inference to the best explanation (Pardo and Allen 2008). Why is that? Because evidentiary arguments are constructed and received under factual uncertainty (Redmayne 2006).

---

[3] For a variety of views, see Bongiovanni et al. (2018). Two classics are MacCormick (1978) and Golding (1980). See also Alchourrón (1996), Sartor (2005), Posner (2008), and Schauer (2009).

As an additional aspect, reasoning is performed when evidence is assessed to determine its probative value. According to "atomistic" models of evidence assessment, fact-finders have to consider each piece of evidence in its own right, to determine its admissibility and, if admitted, its probative value. According to "holistic" models, fact-finders need to consider the whole amount of evidence at their disposal, for it is often the case that single pieces of evidence cannot prove a claim that can be proven when taken together. Next, once the evidence is assessed, fact-finders need to consider whether it meets the relevant standard of proof. In Anglo-American legal systems, the traditional standard in criminal cases is proof beyond a reasonable doubt; in civil cases, it is the preponderance of evidence, or balance of probabilities. The criminal standard requires an amount of evidence that only leaves room for unreasonable doubts about the defendant's guilt. If the evidence presented and assessed makes it reasonable to believe that the defendant is guilty and makes it unreasonable to doubt it, then the prosecution is entitled to a verdict in its favor and the fact-finders are committed to decide against the defendant. Instead, in civil cases the fact-finders are supposed to decide for the party whose claim is better supported by the evidence which was presented and assessed. If the plaintiff claims to have been harmed by the defendant, fact-finders are supposed to decide for the plaintiff if there is a preponderance of the evidence in favor of the plaintiff's claim; otherwise they must decide for the defendant. In the version of the standard that explicitly uses probabilities, the party whose claim appears to be more probable given the evidence is entitled to a decision in its favor. Over the last years the literature on this topic has significantly grown. Suffice it to say that, on the one hand, qualitative formulas like "beyond a reasonable doubt" need interpretation and that, on the other hand, quantitative accounts in probability terms run the risk of artificial precision. As to the first problem, what do we mean by "reasonable" doubt? How can we tell reasonable from unreasonable doubts? With regard to the second problem, for example, how can we translate the testimony of a witness into probabilities? Using subjective probabilities is a poor solution in this domain, since parties and fact-finders are supposed to provide *reasons* for the assessment of evidence; they are not supposed to disclose their mere preferences or subjective probabilities.

In the second place, legal reasoning is about the *norms* that govern a case. These norms can be legal rules, standards, or principles. The basic problem is that decision-makers do not find norms as such. What they usually have is a bunch of authoritative texts, materials, and precedents, and the norms provided by these sources can be unclear or disputed. According to some authors, in most cases the directives of action provided by legal sources are clear, and no interpretation is needed (Marmor 2005, making a distinction between interpretation and understanding). So, at least in the cases just mentioned, judges are not required to perform a specific kind of reasoning to identify the rule of the case. They simply understand what the law says. On the contrary, others claim that legal sources are always in need of interpretation, given the complexity of legal systems, the indeterminacy of legal language, and the fact that the content of legal sources is disputable even when it is clear (see Guastini 2004; as for the disputability of a legal answer when the law is clear, see Endicott 1996). Even in the easiest cases—so the argument goes—legal practitioners make interpretative choices with regard to the sources to be considered, their content, and the circumstance that a given interpretation is suitable to the case. In this view, therefore, norms are not the input but the output of the interpretive process. The input is constituted by the provisions, materials, and precedents the process starts with.

As it may be, legal practitioners are supposed to provide arguments that justify the choice of the norm to be applied to the case. Parties provide these reasons in the first place; then judges are supposed to evaluate them, to make decisions on the litigated points, and to justify their decisions.[4] What we call *first-order arguments* about the interpretation and application of law are used to support these claims, both by parties and judges. The contemporary theories of legal interpretation and argumentation (e.g. Alexy 1978; Tarello 1980; MacCormick and Summers 1991; Guastini 2004; Walton et al. 2018) distinguish several such arguments, notably the following[5]:

---

[4] In general, judges are not bound by the arguments given by the parties, in the sense that they are not required by the law to ground their rulings on them. Yet, the arguments provided by the parties are usually the starting point of judicial reasoning, the materials from which judges draw up their decisions.

[5] The lists of arguments differ to some extent. For instance, Walton et al. (2018, pp. 521–522) distinguish the following: (1) argument from ordinary meaning, (2) argument from technical meaning, (3) argument from contextual harmonization, (4) argument from precedent, (5) argument from statutory analogy, (6) argument from a legal concept, (7) argument from general principles, (8) argument from history, (9) argument from purpose, (10) argument from substantive reasons, and (11) argument from intention.

1. *Literal arguments*, or arguments from wording
2. *A contrario arguments*, or arguments from the silence of legislature
3. *Psychological arguments*, or arguments from legislative intention
4. *Teleological arguments*, or arguments from purpose
5. *A simili arguments*, or arguments from analogy
6. *Arguments from precedent*
7. *Systemic arguments*, or arguments from systemic coherence
8. *Arguments from principle*
9. *Arguments from equity*

All these arguments extract normative content from authoritative sources, namely from legal texts that are in need of interpretation and application to actual cases. And some of the listed arguments, especially the arguments from analogy, have an integrative function, since they fill in the gaps in the law. Typically, integrative arguments point at some relevant similarities or dissimilarities between cases, under the general principle that similar cases should be treated alike and different cases should be treated differently. For instance, analogy performs this integrative role by claiming that the unregulated case is relevantly similar to a regulated one and therefore should be treated alike.

It is not always easy to distinguish one argument from another, and to appreciate its role. A significant example of this is the controversial relationship between psychological and teleological arguments (see Sartor 2002; Westerman 2010). Some legal scholars claim, in particular, that in EU law the former are less important than the latter, since EU directives are formulated in terms of goals and objectives to achieve. Some add that teleological arguments are "objective" while psychological ones are merely "subjective". For the very same reason other scholars claim that it is not important to argue about goals, when these are already stated by legislative authorities. Pauline Westerman has claimed, in particular, that "goal-regulation can be understood as a complete reversal of the traditional state of affairs, in which rules fix and prescribe a certain course of action to be followed in order to reach a certain goal. … In goal-regulation that relationship is reversed. The goals are fixed and the means are left undetermined" (Westerman 2010, p. 216). In her opinion, "most of the teleological interpretation necessarily turns into historical interpretation, focusing on the aims and purposes of the various legislators involved. This limitation affects the kind of arguments that are put forward as justification for decisions. Only explicit aims have justificatory power" (Westerman

2010, p. 222). If so, arguments from *purpose* convert into arguments from *intention* (or "historical" arguments). But one may still claim that the very point of such legislative efforts is to focus on goals rather than on intentions.

Arguments from *economic consequences* are of special interest for law and economics scholars. The basic idea is to justify (or criticize) a decision on the basis of its economic consequences, actual or expected. However, in legal practice such arguments are usually presented under different headings, as arguments from (economic) purpose or arguments from (economic) intention (see Cserne 2020). This is not surprising when one realizes that, to have justificatory power in law, such consequences must be *legally relevant* (Esposito and Tuzet 2020)—namely, relevant to a legislative purpose or intent, or relevant to the implementation of a policy or the promotion of a principle.[6] Of course, there is more room for economic considerations in lawmaking activities such as legislation.

One has also to consider the *argumentative structures* that parties and judges use to justify their claims. Almost always more than one argument is used. Then arguments are arranged in convergence- or chain-structures. In the former some independent arguments lead to the same conclusion. In the latter the conclusion of one argument is a premise of another. It is an empirical matter whether parties and judges reason more often according to convergence- or chain-structures. For sure, one advantage of a convergence-structure is that the conclusion may still hold in case one of the convergent arguments is rejected.

Unfortunately, it is often the case that one argument pulls in one direction and another in a different one. For instance, arguments from wording and from purpose frequently conflict in hard cases. Then decision-makers need *second-order arguments* which provide preference rules employed to prefer an argument over another. Such preference rules are based on normative conceptions of interpretation as value-oriented (Wróblewski 1992, pp. 61ff). The need for those rules follows from the fact that very frequently the conflicting standpoints are supported by different arguments. In principle, for any legal argument there is a possible counterargument (Llewellyn 1950). As a typical controversy, one party advocates a literal interpretation of a normative text and the other party contends that the

---

[6] The notion of relevance is a tricky one. Suffice it here to say that some consequences are "legally relevant" if they meet some legal *desiderata*. In this sense, legal relevance is not to be confused with logical, political, or economic relevance.

text must be interpreted in a purposive way. If such arguments lead to opposite conclusions, the decision-maker needs a reason to prefer one over another.

Interestingly, Richard Posner has claimed that economic considerations can play a significant role when judges have *discretion*: courts can be legitimately guided by economic considerations (wealth maximization in Posner's own view) "where the Constitution or legislation does not deprive them of initiative or discretion in the matter" (1985, p. 103). This counts as using economic arguments as first-order ones when preexisting law does not rule the matter.[7] But similarly, judges can use economic arguments as second-order ones when first-order arguments conflict and the economic considerations can tip the scales in favor of one of the first-order arguments.

It is sensible to claim that in criminal law textual or literal arguments should prevail over others because they put more constraints on judicial interpretation and decision-making and therefore better protect the rights of criminal defendants. If a legal system has an *interpretive directive* that dictates the preference for one argument over another, such a directive can be used as a second-order argument, whereas the arguments in the ranking are first-order ones. Second-order arguments apply the systemic preference criteria about first-order ones. More precisely, they concern the precedence of some argument when they require it to be used before others; and they concern the prevalence of it when they require that, in case of conflict between outcomes generated by different arguments, one argument be given more weight or strength. The precedence relation is usually accompanied by the idea that the subsequent arguments need not come into play if the precedent ones are sufficient to settle the issue.

On the one hand, some legal systems provide explicit lists of first-order arguments (e.g. art. 12 of the preliminary provisions of the 1942 Italian Civil Code, art. 3 of the 1889 Spanish Civil Code, § 7 of the Austrian "General Civil Code" of 1811). On the other hand, it is very hard to find in positive law explicit indications of second-order arguments. One may claim that, in criminal law, a strict literal interpretation should in general prevail over other arguments and considerations. But one can also find

---

[7]For more details on Posner's views, see Cserne (2020). On "discretion" suffice it to say that judges have discretion when the law does not already regulate a certain issue; then they are expected to adjudicate it according to prudence as practical wisdom (Hart 2013), or to principles (Dworkin 1978, 1985), or to other valuable considerations such as economic ones.

several cases where the latter are found to prevail (see, for example, Canale and Tuzet 2017). There are tendencies in legal practice that amount to implicit second-order arguments, and as such those tendencies are susceptible to many exceptions depending on the specific context and stakes.

To give an example, if the law considers as an aggravating circumstance of an offence the "use of a firearm" during and in relation to a drug-trafficking crime, does this encompass the exchange of an automatic weapon for cocaine? In Smith v. U.S. (U.S. Supreme Court, 1993) the starting argument against the defendant was that "use of a firearm" literally encompasses *any* use of a firearm that facilitates the commission of a drug offence, including the use of it as an item of barter. Against this argument the defense pointed out that, in a contextual understanding of language, when we refer to the use of an artifact we refer to the standard or intended use of it (the use the artifact was created for). Therefore, so the argument went, the relevant "use of a firearm" would be the use of it *as a weapon* and in the case in hand the defendant didn't use it as such, for he tried to employ it as a means of payment. Against the defendant it was also pointed out that the legislative purpose was to minimize the risk that the presence of drugs and firearms imposes on individuals and society. Drugs and guns are a dangerous combination and, the argument went, any use of a firearm during and in relation to a drug-trafficking crime should be sanctioned in order to minimize that risk. Now, the argumentation theorist can apply to this case the categories mentioned earlier and claim that the convergent combination of the first literal argument and the argument from purpose outweighed, in the final decision, the second literal argument, namely the argument from contextual meaning advanced in favor of the defendant. The defendant was sentenced to a significant prison term.

2.3   A MODEL AND ITS ENHANCEMENT: THE JUDICIAL SYLLOGISM AND THE DOUBLE JUSTIFICATION MODEL

Analytic theorists typically divide legal arguments into two broad categories: arguments about *facts* and arguments about *norms*. Arguments about facts, as already pointed out, aim at justifying (or contesting) the reconstruction of the relevant facts. Parties typically produce evidence to support their factual claims, or to contest rival claims. And given that evidence *per se* doesn't yield verdicts, the evidence presented is in need of being "inferentialized", that is translated into evidentiary inferences and arguments aimed at persuading the fact-finders. Arguments about norms aim at justifying (or contesting) the identification and application of legal norms. Parties typically discuss about a legal provision which one of them at least considers to be relevant and applicable to the case in hand. The provision is usually in need of interpretation, or of being contextualized to the system or subsystem it belongs to. The latter operation requires a reconstruction of the system, of its parts, principles, statutory norms, relevant judicial precedents, and so on.

Once the facts are found and the relevant norms are identified, the decision-makers need only apply the latter to the former. For some analytic approaches this kind of application consists, logically speaking, in a deductive inference. According to the traditional model of the *judicial syllogism*, decision-makers are to deduce the outcome of the case from the facts and the applicable norms. The model was advanced by Cesare Beccaria in his 1764 masterpiece *Dei delitti e delle pene* (Chap. IV). It was meant as a normative model to constrain judicial decision-making in criminal law. It was not presented as a model descriptive of judicial practice. In fact, Beccaria was quite critical of the criminal justice system of his time. His main critique concentrated on the arbitrariness of criminal decision-making in his days. As a remedy to it, he recommended that judges decide according to a syllogism model, with a general legal norm provided by legislation as major premise, the relevant fact as minor premise, and the outcome as a logical deductive conclusion.

To make a very simple illustration (of course actual cases are far more complex), if legislation establishes that whoever does A shall be punished with S (major premise), and if Basil did A (minor premise), then Basil shall be punished with S (conclusion). The argument has a deductive logical structure: if the premises are true, the conclusion cannot be false. Or, the conclusion is necessarily correct given the correctness of the premises. The model preserves legal certainty (or the rule of law), as well as the principle of equal treatment under the law: if Basil did A and whoever does A shall be punished with S, not punishing him with S would be to treat him differently. Deductive application of law permits to treat like cases alike.

The model can be extended from criminal to civil matters. If legislation establishes that whoever wrongfully harms another person shall compensate this person (major premise), and Basil wrongfully harmed Theodor (minor premise), then Basil shall compensate Theodor (conclusion). Again, the argument has a deductive logical structure in that the conclusion cannot be false if the premises are true. And again, it preserves legal certainty and equality. Both logical and legal principles support the model.

But judges need reasons to assume the premises of the syllogism. They do not find the premises as one finds mushrooms under the trees. The premises must be determined out of the relevant legal sources and evidence. Parties present arguments whose conclusions are possible premises of the judicial syllogism. Then adjudicators evaluate their arguments and, if needed, supplement them. So, as many critics have pointed out, the syllogism model is too simple in this respect. One needs arguments *for the premises*. In fact, the vast majority of legal disputes concern such arguments.

That calls for an enhancement of the model. A well-established view in the contemporary literature has it that the justification of judicial decisions is double: internal and external. We call "internal" the justification of the conclusion provided by the deductive structure of the syllogism, and "external" the justification of its premises.[8] On the whole, we can call this the *double justification model*.

In turn, external justification has two aspects. Interpretive and integrative arguments provide the external justification of the major premise of the syllogism, and evidentiary arguments provide the external justification of its minor premise. Both aspects, normative and factual external justification, may be determined by first- and second-order arguments. As simple illustrations, imagine a context where literal meaning prevails over purposive meaning and a context where scientific testimony prevails over a lay one. In such contexts some second-order arguments dispose of the conflicts between first-order ones. Then, once the premises are established along such lines, the syllogism provides the internal justification of the outcome. If it has been normatively established that whoever wrongfully harms another person shall compensate this person, and it has been proven that Basil wrongfully harmed Theodor, then Basil shall compensate Theodor. The conclusion has a double justification if both premises and conclusion of the reasoning are justified.

In its typical structure, normative external justification goes from provisions to norms through interpretive (or integrative) arguments (see § 2 earlier). In its typical structure, factual external justification goes from evidence to factual reconstruction through "bridge rules". Bridge rules are empirical generalizations, scientific laws, and legal rules concerning the

---

[8] See Wróblewski (1971, 1974); Alexy (1978). Cf. MacCormick (1978) for similar points.

probative value of the evidence. Bridge rules connect the evidence at disposal with the relevant facts as they can be reconstructed (again, see § 2 earlier). Jerzy Wróblewski (1971, p. 415) distinguishes in this respect "rules of empirical evidence" and "rules of legal evidence", to account for the various ways (our "bridge rules") in which evidence leads to the facts to be proven; a rule of the first kind can be a rule of common sense, a rule of the second kind a legal presumption. In a partially different account, bridge rules connect secondary to primary facts. Secondary facts are the probatory facts evidence amounts to (e.g. the fact that witness W said that p); primary facts are the facts to be proven, namely the legally relevant facts (whether it was the case that p); and bridge rules justify the reasoning from the ones to the others (being W a reliable witness, it can be inferred that p). Fact-finders assess the evidence along such lines and decide according to the standard of proof.

From a logical point of view, one can conceive of normative external justification as deductive if one considers interpretive arguments as directives that, like normative major premises, shall be applied to the interpretive problem at hand (then one has to solve, with second-order arguments, the possible conflicts between such directives). Or, one can look at normative external justification as the epistemic effort to find the best interpretation for the case in hand. This is possible if one considers interpretive arguments as heuristic devices that help interpreters find the correct or best interpretation of the relevant materials for the case in hand. Logically speaking, in this sense, normative external justification becomes abductive, or a form of inference to the best explanation, being an educated guess at what is most correct in legal terms. Factual external justification is more straightforwardly epistemic, even if some bridge rules have a legal nature and the standards of proof respond to principles and values. From a logical point of view, factual external justification is mainly abductive; or, more generally speaking, it is the effort to find the best explanation of the evidence and to check whether it satisfies the relevant standard of proof.

REFERENCES

Alchourrón, Carlos E. 1996. On Law and Logic. *Ratio Juris* 9: 331–348.

Alexy, Robert. 1978. *Theorie der juristischen Argumentation. Die Theorie des rationalen Diskurses als Theorie der juristischen Begründung.* Frankfurt am Main: Suhrkamp. Engl. ed. 1989. *A Theory of Legal Argumentation.* Oxford: Clarendon Press.

Anderson, Terence, David Schum, and William Twining. 2005. *Analysis of Evidence*. 2nd ed. Cambridge: Cambridge University Press.

Bongiovanni, Giorgio, Gerald Postema, Antonino Rotolo, Giovanni Sartor, Chiara Valentini, and Douglas Walton, eds. 2018. *Handbook of Legal Reasoning and Argumentation*. Dordrecht: Springer.

Canale, Damiano, and Giovanni Tuzet. 2017. Analogical Reasoning and Extensive Interpretation. *Archiv für Rechts- und Sozialphilosophie* 103: 117–135. Reprinted in *Analogy and Exemplary Reasoning in Legal Discourse*, ed. Hendrik Kaptein and Bastiaan van der Velden, 65–86. Amsterdam: Amsterdam University Press, 2018.

Comanducci, Paolo. 2000. Ragionamento giuridico. In *I metodi della giustizia civile*, ed. Mario Bessone, Elisabetta Silvestri, and Michele Taruffo, 79–136. Padova: Cedam.

Cserne, Péter. 2020. Economic Approaches to Legal Reasoning: An Overview. In *Economics in Legal Reasoning*, ed. Péter Cserne and Fabrizio Esposito, 25–41. London: Palgrave Macmillan.

Dworkin, Ronald. 1978. *Taking Rights Seriously*. Cambridge: Harvard University Press.

———. 1985. *A Matter of Principle*. Cambridge: Harvard University Press.

Endicott, Timothy A.O. 1996. Linguistic Indeterminacy. *Oxford Journal of Legal Studies* 16: 667–697.

Esposito, Fabrizio, and Giovanni Tuzet. 2020. Economic Consequences as Legal Values: A Legal Inferentialist Approach. In *Law and Economics as Interdisciplinary Exchange. Philosophical, Methodological and Historical Perspectives*, ed. Péter Cserne and Magdalena Małecka, 135–157. Abingdon: Routledge.

Ferrer, Jordi. 2007. *La valoración racional de la prueba*. Madrid: Marcial Pons.

Golding, Martin P. 1980. *Legal Reasoning*. New York: Random House.

Guastini, Riccardo. 2004. *L'interpretazione dei documenti normativi*. Milano: Giuffrè.

Haack, Susan. 2014. *Evidence Matters. Science, Proof, and Truth in the Law*. Cambridge: Cambridge University Press.

Hart, Herbert L.A. 2013. Discretion. *Harvard Law Review* 127: 652–665.

Llewellyn, Karl N. 1950. Remarks on the Theory of Appellate Decision and The Rules or Canons about How Statutes are to be Construed. *Vanderbilt Law Review* 3: 395–406.

MacCormick, Neil. 1978. *Legal Reasoning and Legal Theory*. Oxford: Oxford University Press. 2nd ed. 1994.

MacCormick, Neil, and Robert Summers, eds. 1991. *Interpreting Statutes*. Aldershot: Ashgate-Dartmouth.

Marmor, Andrei. 2005. *Interpretation and Legal Theory. Revised Second Edition*. Oxford: Hart.

Pardo, Michael S., and Ronald J. Allen. 2008. Juridical Proof and the Best Explanation. *Law and Philosophy* 27: 223–268.

Posner, Richard A. 1985. Wealth Maximization Revisited. *Notre Dame Journal of Ethics and Public Policy* 2: 85–105.

———. 2008. *How Judges Think*. Cambridge and London: Harvard University Press.

Redmayne, Mike. 2006. The Structure of Evidence Law. *Oxford Journal of Legal Studies* 26: 805–822.

Sartor, Giovanni. 2002. Teleological Arguments and Theory-Based Dialectics. *Artificial Intelligence and Law* 10: 95–112.

———. 2005. *Legal Reasoning. A Cognitive Approach to the Law*. Dordrecht: Springer.

Schauer, Frederick. 2009. *Thinking Like a Lawyer. A New Introduction to Legal Reasoning*. Cambridge and London: Harvard University Press.

Tarello, Giovanni. 1980. *L'interpretazione della legge*. Milano: Giuffrè.

Tuzet, Giovanni. 2003. Legal Abductions. In *Legal Knowledge and Information Systems: Jurix 2003*, ed. Danielle Bourcier, 41–49. Amsterdam: IOS Press.

Twining, William. 1990. *Rethinking Evidence. Exploratory Essays*. Oxford: Blackwell. 2nd ed. 2006. Cambridge: Cambridge University Press.

Walton, Douglas. 2018. Legal Reasoning and Argumentation. In *Handbook of Legal Reasoning and Argumentation*, ed. G. Bongiovanni et al., 47–75. Dordrecht: Springer.

Walton, Douglas, Giovanni Sartor, and Fabrizio Macagno. 2018. Statutory Interpretation as Argumentation. In *Handbook of Legal Reasoning and Argumentation*, ed. G. Bongiovanni et al., 519–560. Dordrecht: Springer.

Westerman, P. 2010. Arguing about Goals. *Argumentation* 24: 211–226.

Wintgens, Luc J., and Daniel Oliver-Lalana, eds. 2013. *The Rationality and Justification of Legislation*. Dordrecht: Springer.

Wróblewski, Jerzy. 1971. Leal Decision and Its Justification. *Logique et Analyse* 14: 409–419.

———. 1974. Legal Syllogism and Rationality of Judicial Decision. *Rechtstheorie* 5: 33–46.

———. 1992. *The Judicial Application of Law*. Dordrecht: Kluwer.

CHAPTER 3

Economic Approaches to Legal Reasoning: An Overview

Péter Cserne

Abstract Economic analysis has contributed to a better understanding and a better functioning of law at different levels of generality. As far as legal reasoning is concerned, these contributions fall into two large groups. Economics in legal reasoning concerns arguments about the purposes and consequences of legal rules and principles that are acceptable in court as legally relevant, including (1) predictions of the likely consequences of alternative legal decisions; (2) technical normative arguments about the best means to achieve a legally determined purpose; and (3) welfarist normative arguments about the desirable goals of specific laws. Economics of legal reasoning, in turn, includes (1) explanatory models of legal processes in terms of rational activity of individuals, corporate entities as well as legal officials, and (2) normative proposals concerning the design of legal processes, that is the structure of law as institutional practice.

P. Cserne (✉)
University of Aberdeen, Aberdeen, UK
e-mail: peter.cserne@abdn.ac.uk

25

© The Author(s) 2020
P. Cserne, F. Esposito (eds.), *Economics in Legal Reasoning*,
Palgrave Studies in Institutions, Economics and Law,
https://doi.org/10.1007/978-3-030-40168-9_3

Keywords Economics in legal reasoning • Economics of legal reasoning • Wealth maximization • Consequence-based arguments • Teleological reasoning • Economics of legal process

3.1   INTRODUCTION

Legal reasoning remains the aspect of legal systems least explored by economists. At first blush, economists tend to denigrate legal reasoning as "mere rhetoric": obfuscation at worst and irrelevant noise or *façon de parler* at best. What matters is the outcome of the proceedings (Is the defendant guilty and punished? Is he liable to pay damages?) or, more generally, how expected legal consequences change human behavior. This functionalist stance leaves little room for analyzing legal reasoning in terms of procedures, reasons, rights and duties.[1]

Economics can nonetheless contribute to legal reasoning in two main ways: first, under the terms set by legal practice. Law and economics scholars accept these terms, at least implicitly, when recognizing that the practical impact of their findings is conditional upon certain characteristics of particular political communities or legal systems. As Sect. 3.2 will argue, the shortest way for economics to enter legal reasoning is in the guise of prudential or consequence-based arguments. The efficiency-based recommendations as to how judges should decide cases and interpret or reform rules are relevant *in* legal reasoning to the extent that teleological or consequence-based arguments are relevant for the justification of legal decisions.

Second, economics also draws attention to and sheds light on aspects of legal reasoning that are not readily explicable, perhaps not even visible, from the perspective of legal practitioners. The institutional forms of legal reasoning in adjudication, or dispute resolution more broadly, display regularities as well as unintended systemic consequences that require analysis: identification, measurement and explanation. Legal processes are also subject to evaluation in light of normative criteria external to them. From this perspective, economics provides tools for decision-makers to evaluate possible reforms. External economic analyses *of* legal reasoning are discussed in Sect. 3.3.

---

[1] More recently, decision-theoretical models aiming at integrating preferences and reasons have been put forward (Dietrich and List 2013).

3.2 ECONOMICS IN LEGAL REASONING: FROM WEALTH MAXIMIZATION TO CONSEQUENCE-BASED ADJUDICATION

Orthodox law and economics scholars once argued vigorously that the common law displays an economic logic: judges should and in effect tend to decide cases such as to maximize social welfare or "wealth" (measured in terms of willingness to pay). "Wealth maximization" has been famously proposed as a positive and normative theory of common law adjudication by Richard Posner (1983, chapters 3 and 4). His proposal has been discussed extensively in both economic models and jurisprudential critique (Kornhauser 1980, 2018b, pp. 718–723).

In spite of impressive partial analyses (e.g. Posner 1972), wealth maximization is not a plausible *positive* theory of adjudication at the level of judicial reasoning or even judicial behavior. Economic efficiency does not generally find a place among acceptable justifications for judicial decisions. It may have a place in the motivations of judges, for example because of nineteenth-century *laissez-faire* ideologies, but there is no systematic evidence for this across times and jurisdictions. However, the positive theory does not hinge on either of these mechanisms. "The efficiency of legal rules might result from processes other than the reasoning of judges" (Kornhauser 2018b, p. 711). Starting with Rubin (1977) and Priest (1977), economists have suggested a range of explanatory theories that identify mechanisms for the evolution of judge-made law (case selection, incentives to litigate, etc.) and/or identify and measure the macroeconomic effects of common law adjudication.[2]

Wealth maximization as a *normative* theory of adjudication, in its simplest formulation, refers to the idea that judges should decide cases such as to maximize social welfare or efficiency. By Posner's own admission (1990, chapter 12, 2007a, pp. 11–12), the fierce jurisprudential and philosophical criticisms of his proposal (Symposium 1980; Dworkin 1980) led him to refine and confine his argument for wealth maximization.[3] Limited

---

[2] Rubin (2007) provides a representative selection. As these positive theories do not assume that judges are motivated by, let alone argue in terms of, efficiency, and as they are not addressed to judges, they represent an external economic perspective on legal reasoning, to be discussed in Sect. 3.3.

[3] Thus, he remarked that the proposal was made in his academic rather than judicial capacity, as "speculation rather than a blueprint for social action" (Posner 1983, p. vi), and acknowledged that "there is more to justice than efficiency" (Posner 2007b, p. 27). For the last 30 years, he has advocated a broader stance of "pragmatic adjudication" (Posner 1990,

versions of efficiency-based theories of adjudication have nonetheless been defended by moral and political philosophers (Coleman 1992; Farber 2000; Kraus 2002). And even if efficiency is not plausible as a norm for individual judges, it may be defensible as a systemic goal: "a requirement that courts announce efficient rules does not entail that judges should adopt an economic logic. Given the structure of adjudication, judges might better achieve efficiency by aiming at something else" (Kornhauser 2018b, p. 711).

The role of economics in legal reasoning goes well beyond wealth maximization. Analytically speaking, all goal-oriented (teleological) legal reasoning follows an economic logic: it is "virtually co-extensive with economic or rational choice reasoning. Teleological reasoning directs the agent, given her ends, to do the best she can. [...] A legal actor engaged in teleological reasoning must first identify her ends, then identify feasible policies that promote those ends, and finally choose the means that best promote those ends" (Kornhauser 2018a, pp. 400, 410). Teleological reasoning appears in law at all levels. Explicitly goal-oriented legislation has been on the rise in many jurisdictions (Westerman 2018). Consequence-based thinking is the bread and butter of cost–benefit analyses supporting administrative agency decisions. The main doctrinal gateway for economic arguments to enter adjudication is consequence-based arguments in legal interpretation.

The rest of this section will focus on consequence-based legal interpretation.[4] It can be roughly characterized thus: if in deciding case C, the decision-maker finds that there is a relevant rule R which has more than one plausible interpretation (X, Y, Z, ...), the decision-maker is said to use a consequence-based argument if she/he justifies her/his decision for rule interpretation X (instead of rule interpretation Y or Z) with the argument that rule interpretation X will bring about consequences which are normatively superior to the consequences brought about by the alternative rule interpretations.

---

chapter 15) which assigns a limited role to economic arguments. Posner's version of pragmatic adjudication seems capable of encompassing the broadest possible set of considerations, including rule-consequentialist arguments for formalist decision-making in certain areas of law or ranks of the judicial hierarchy. A later round of foundational debates on normative law and economics, initiated by Kaplow and Shavell (2002), had little direct impact on theories of legal reasoning.

[4] The rest of this section relies on and updates Cserne (2011).

While a judicial decision is mostly backward-looking in the sense of adjudicating about a set of facts that happened in the past, it is sometimes justified with reference to the future.[5] When judges are authorized to base their decision on consequential considerations, they also have the duty to justify their decision with arguments related to the expected consequences of alternative rulings. As far as legal reasoning is concerned, consequences only matter to the extent that they are explicitly referred to in public justificatory arguments. In various jurisdictions, "prudential arguments" (Craswell 1993, p. 293), policy arguments (Bell 1995) or consequence-based reasoning (Teubner 1995) have been accepted in adjudication (Lieth 2007, Carbonell Bellolio 2011). Whether such reasoning can be recast as arguments from "subjective" legislative intention or from "objective" purpose, or falls under a different category of the canon depends on the acceptability and weight of those kinds of arguments in particular legal cultures, domains and disputes.

The notion of consequences needs to be specified. First, we may distinguish 'juridical' and 'behavioral' consequences (Rudden 1979, p. 194). Juridical consequences are internal to the legal system: the judge examines the logical implications of interpretation X or Y on other rules within the legal system, by inquiring "what sorts of conduct the rule would authorize or proscribe" (MacCormick 1983, p. 239). Behavioral consequences refer to "what human behavior the rule will induce or discourage" outside the legal system, in society at large (MacCormick 1983, p. 239).

We may further distinguish individual and systemic behavioral consequences. The first concern the parties involved in an individual case. For instance, judges often decide about the detention of a criminal suspect based on the likelihood that the suspect will escape or commit further crimes. A higher court may also realize that a broader or narrower construction of the doctrine of causation would have an impact on medical liability throughout the legal system and society, for example it may lead to "defensive medicine" or shortage in medical services (Cane 2000,

---

[5] While the consequences of a legal decision can be related to the decision in several ways, not all figure consequence-based reasoning. Courts, especially higher or constitutional courts, often take decisions with large-scale social consequences. This does not mean that judges are necessarily aware of these consequences or that, if they are, their decisions will be motivated by what they expect to result from their decision. Even if, as a matter of psychology, they are influenced by the expected consequences, they are not always willing or allowed to publicly refer to them as reasons for their decision.

p. 45). When judges consider the impact of their decision on the rules of civil liability, on similar tort cases in the future, or on the conduct of potential injurers and victims, *and* justify their decision with reference to such considerations, they are said to use general or systemic consequence-based arguments.

When judges refer to behavioral consequences, they make a more or less educated guess about how certain groups of legal subjects would change their behavior in response to a certain decision. In order to do this, they have to imagine and compare hypothetical scenarios under the assumption that individuals will change their behavior in a predictable way, in response to how the law would regulate their dealings. To deal with behavioral consequences, the decision-maker needs, first, information and a behavioral theory as to how the interpretation of the rule will induce behavioral changes, and, second, normative standards to compare states of the world that various decisions are expected to bring about.[6] While judges often use nothing more than intuition and introspection in predicting behavioral consequences, there are good reasons for them to rely on systematic data and explicit theories. While not all consequence-based arguments are economic, a judicial argument based on an expected improvement in efficiency or social welfare is an argument based on behavioral consequences. In fact, typical arguments of *law and economics* are based on such consequences. Economics as a social science plays a role in predicting behavioral consequences. Welfare economics provides normative standards to evaluate those consequences. The so-called efficiency theory of the common law discussed above is *par excellence* a consequentialist position both in the sense that it requires judges to base their decisions on consequences, namely their effect on social welfare, and in the sense that it is usually backed by a consequentialist moral theory, namely wealth maximization.

Although economists do not carefully distinguish whether they consider contributing to moral or legal discourse, and Posner's theory of law is properly characterized as consequentialist in both senses (White and Patterson 1999, pp. 94–95), one should nonetheless distinguish consequentialism as a moral theory (Pettit 1991) and consequence-based

---

[6] Obviously, evaluating interpretative choices based on juridical consequences also requires normative standards. On how to choose normative standards suggested in economics and/ or to identify those implicit in legal reasoning, see Esposito and Tuzet (2019) and Esposito (2020).

arguments in legal reasoning. This distinction emphasizes the relative autonomy of legal reasoning. Logically speaking, consequence-based legal reasoning neither requires nor implies consequentialism as a substantive moral standpoint (Barnett 1989, p. 43). In particular instances, formalistic (backward-looking, rule-based) legal reasoning may lead to (morally or economically) better consequences overall than consequentialist adjudication.

Schematically, a consequence-based judicial decision (a teleological argument) can be represented as a three-step procedure of optimization under uncertainty: first, identify the relevant normative standard(s); second, measure the consequences of each possible decision in the dimensions indicated by the standard(s); third, weight and compare the possible decisions and choose the one with the overall best expected consequences (Table 3.1).

Ideally, a fully informed rational decision-maker can solve the problem of consequence-based decision-making in an optimal way.[7] Real-world judges run into serious difficulties at each step. First, the judge has to identify which consequences of her/his decision are relevant. Some of these effects are easy to identify or even quantify, at least in theory. Others are notoriously difficult to operationalize. For instance, when it comes to economic goals of specific doctrines or areas of law such as efficiency, welfare, cost minimization or market integration, even their identification is controversial.[8]

Second, the judge has to measure the impact of her/his decision in all dimensions identified and operationalized in step one. Here she/he faces severe information imperfections and fundamental uncertainty about

Table 3.1 Three steps of consequence-based reasoning

Step	Question to be answered by the decision-maker	Difficulties
1. Identification	Which consequences (effects) matter?	Operationalization
2. Measurement	What is the impact of the decision?	Information
3. Evaluation	Which decision has better consequences overall?	Trade-offs

[7] Here, we disregard complications of sequential and strategic decision-making—for these, as well as for a formal model of consequential reasoning, see Kornhauser (2018a).

[8] On the identification of the goal of particular laws, with special reference to different conceptions of social welfare, see Esposito (2020).

certain relevant variables, including both facts and the causal mechanisms leading to facts. The unpredictability of potential consequences is a standard criticism of consequentialism as an ethical theory. *Mutatis mutandis*, it applies to legal reasoning as well. To apply this standard literally in a judicial choice between alternative rule interpretations would make the role impossible to fulfill. Even a perfectly conscientious Herculean judge, with unconstrained time and the best expertise, would have to face limits of information and foresight, at least because of the inherent uncertainty of the future. In most real-world settings, judges have a predominantly legal training and have limited access to expertise to undertake complex probability calculations or full-blown statistical analyses. The information required or admitted is limited by rules of evidence. Epistemic considerations compete with other criteria: "the law" as a practice cannot be suspended until the best theoretical solutions are found or all the relevant consequences of a decision are carefully examined. Hence, even available information may not be processed in a systematic and theoretically sound way.[9]

Third, when choosing between alternatives, the judge has to evaluate the overall consequences of possible decisions in light of relevant normative standards. If those consequences cannot be easily reduced to or measured in a single dimension, the assessment involves trade-offs. The expected consequences have to be evaluated and, whether or not this is called "balancing", value-laden trade-offs have to be made (Petersen 2017). This means that consequence-based decisions are not merely technical, neutral or "objective" in the sense of being merely factual.

As Kornhauser argued:

> One common attack on teleological reasoning in law rests on its extreme difficulty. Determination of the consequences of a policy is extremely difficult. [...] One might circumvent the difficulty of predicting distant and complex consequences by adopting a different set of criteria against which to assess institutions or policies. One might, for example, adopt more procedural criteria against which to assess the policy or the institution. Or one might adopt criteria with shorter time horizons. [...] The challenges of teleological reasoning by legal agents do not argue for its abandonment. Legislation enacted without contemplation or concern for the consequences it engenders would be foolish indeed. (Kornhauser 2018a, pp. 409, 408, 410)

Let us briefly consider judicial decision-making in empirical terms. What is likely to happen if a real-world judge has a duty to assess the

---

[9] Some of these issues are discussed in Hubková (2020).

general social consequences of their decision? Research suggests that in case of (radically) insufficient information, time and technical expertise, judicial decisions may still be teleological, and thus consequence-based. Instead of solving a full-blown stochastic optimization problem, decision-makers tend to rely on heuristics and "rules of thumb" (Gigerenzer and Engel 2006). Just as in nonjudicial contexts where "intuitive experts" make millions of complex decisions every day with tolerable results, judges adopt simple decision procedures and routines, and reduce complex decision-making problems into simple ones. For instance, when deciding on detention of criminal suspects (a context which seems to require at least some consequence-based thinking but limits the information and time available for such decisions), judges seem to consider a limited number of variables, and weight these in a simple, predictable way (Dhami 2003).

Most of these mechanisms operate subconsciously (billiard players do not solve complex equations to calculate what to do); thus agents cannot account for their role in their decisions. Yet knowing these heuristics allows observers to predict the decisions. Arguably, in those domains of life where agents are free to decide in unaccountable ways, this is unproblematic. In legal contexts, intuitive or heuristically driven decisions need to be justified with reasonable public arguments: adjudication remains in the domain of discursive rationality (as required by political and moral principles such as the rule of law). As such, the fact that judges tend to rely on heuristics does not relieve them from their role-based duty of justification. Importantly, empirical research also suggests that the duty of justification may improve decision quality in substantive terms (Engel 2004). In brief, representation norms matter.

Closer to our problem, if human decision-makers are authorized to base their reasoning on consequences but lack information and expertise, such a mandate could backfire. An across-the-board mandate for consequence-based reasoning is likely to bring about intuitive, speculative or subjective decisions, eventually disguised as objective and well-founded. Instead of calculative optimization, judges may enter into speculations about the behavioral consequences of their decisions without any serious reliance on empirical evidence. In view of this danger, one might reject consequence-based adjudication altogether and want judges to turn back to non-consequential criteria or "simple rules" (Epstein 1997).[10]

---

[10] As Cane (2000, p. 43) put it, "to the extent that sound empirical support is lacking for arguments about the likely impact of legal rules on human behaviour (i.e. we are ignorant

In fact, based on a combination of epistemic, prudential and moral considerations, economists, mainly in the Austrian and constitutional political economy traditions, argue for a (more) formalist adjudication. They emphasize the benefits of judicial restraint and rule-following in terms of certainty, predictability and, indirectly, economic prosperity; and in other formulations, as a mechanism to enforce individual rights grounded in autonomy (Buchanan 1974; Schwartzstein 1994; Portuese et al. 2018). Thus, epistemic considerations, intertwined with questions of transparency and legitimacy, suggest a limited role for consequentialism in adjudication and provide support for doctrines of judicial restraint. Yet even judges who are expected to reason formalistically are likely to rely on heuristics and fall prey to biases.

This section was concerned with how economics can contribute to legal reasoning from the internal perspective of a lawyer or judge. In order to be intelligible as legal, specifically judicial argument, economic analysis needs to be couched in the form that is acceptable as legally relevant. Whether economically informed adjudication is feasible and desirable in particular contexts will depend on both (1) the psychology of judicial decision-making (Klein and Mitchell 2010) and (2) the incentive effects of formal and informal rules that govern the legal process. The next section will discuss aspects of these incentive effects.

3.3   Economics of Legal Reasoning: Explaining and Designing Legal Processes

While the previous section looked at legal reasoning from a doctrinal perspective, the rules and customs governing legal reasoning can also be analyzed economically, either (1) as instruments for a notional benevolent designer to maximize certain goals (policy perspective) or (2) as variables that change as a result of interest group politics (political economy perspective) (Kornhauser 2017, section 1.3).

Adopting the policy perspective, law and economics scholars provide hypothetical/prudential normative arguments about the best means to achieve certain goals concerning the internal structure of law as institutional practice. Usually they do not question all layers and levels of this complex institutional practice in one step. Most economic analyses of the

about the likely behavioural consequences of legal rules), we need to develop criteria of good decision-making which do not depend upon knowledge of likely consequences".

legal process are partial in the sense that they take most features of the legal process as exogenously given and analyze the effect of changes in a few specific variables as explananda or policy targets. Step by step, the focus of the analysis may broaden, to explore more elements of the institutional context of adjudication. When a mechanism provides partial improvement in one respect, it may carry costs in others as an unintended consequence. Methodologically speaking, the most important contribution of economic analysis to legal reasoning is a systematic exploration of the trade-offs and unintended consequences of planned or actual reforms of procedural rules (Bix 2018, 2019). The analysis is either theoretical, in the form of analytical models, or increasingly empirical using the entire range of quantitative and qualitative methods. This section merely gives a flavor of the general approach and indicates a few themes in this increasingly specialized area.

In what has become the basic economic model of legal procedures, Posner (2007b, pp. 599–600) suggested that the objective of legal process is to minimize the sum of error costs and administrative costs. This simple model provides heuristic rationales for certain features of the legal system as well as generates a number of testable hypotheses.

Assume, for instance, that the expected cost of an accident is $100; the potential injurer can prevent the accident at the cost of $90 (the victim cannot prevent the accident); thus it is efficient to hold the injurer liable (we save $10 of social cost of accidents). If the legal system makes an error in assigning liability in 15% of the cases,[11] then the potential injurer only faces $85 of expected liability. This is less than his/her cost of avoidance; hence if the injurer is a rational cost-minimizer the accident will not be prevented. Assume, further, that we could reduce the error rate of the legal procedure from 15% to 10% at the cost of $20 per accident. This would not be a cost-justified intervention as it would eliminate the error cost (10$) at the expense of $20.

What is the benefit of such a simple model for understanding the legal process? Even if most of these variables cannot be quantified, they allow qualitative comparisons of the expected benefits and costs of various procedural rules. These considerations also matter for institutional design: rationalization, criticism or reform. For instance, Posner (2007b, p. 600) suggests that it is cost-justified to notify the owner and hold a hearing

---

[11] In this simple example, error means "false negatives", that is mistakenly not finding the injurer liable.

before towing and destroying an apparently abandoned car: the potential error cost is much higher than the cost of a hearing. In contrast, a "predeprivation hearing" is not efficient when towing away an illegally parked car: the potential loss is much lower (the car is not destroyed) and the notification would eliminate the deterrent effect of the threat of towing.

Explanatory analyses concerning the incentive effects of legal processes start with the following question. Assuming they cannot recur to brute force, why do rational individual or collective agents litigate and recur to legal processes? For instance, how does the victim of a breach of contract decide whether to sue the other party, settle the dispute or swallow the losses and continue to cooperate? And how do various rules of the legal process impact on this decision? If both parties can predict the court's decision, settling the case by bargaining in the shadow of the law allows them to save the costs of litigation. Yet, if parties have different perceptions of their chance to win (either because one or both are overoptimistic or have private information), this may reduce their willingness to settle. There may be further strategic considerations at play, for example the incentive to build a reputation of toughness and insistence on strict legal rights. Parties may also have preferences that do not coincide with their narrow self-interest or may not calculate rationally. Crucially, the litigation/settlement decision will depend on how the legal process, including the rules governing legal reasoning, is designed: who bears the costs of the process; what kind of evidence is allowed and how it is evaluated; what role are juries, experts (Posner 1999) and advocates (Dewatripont and Tirole 1999) allowed to play. These other actors are expected or "designed" to fulfill specific functions in the legal process while they also pursue their private interests within formal and informal constraints.

These and virtually all aspects of the legal process have been analyzed extensively in the law and economics literature.[12] The literature is also rich in domain-specific analyses that focus on legal reasoning in areas such as constitutional reasoning (Posner 1987; Cooter and Gilbert 2019); statutory interpretation (Ferejohn and Weingast 1992; Cooter and Ginsburg 1996); precedents (Landes and Posner 1976); and contracts (Katz 2004; Posner 2005). As the "point", "purpose" or "function" of these areas differs, there are reasons to share the competence for forward-looking decisions between legislation (rule-setting) and adjudication (rule application) differently and

---

[12] Starting with seminal articles by Landes (1971), Gould (1973) and Posner (1973). For a classic overview, see Cooter and Rubinfeld (1989); see also Tullock (1980).

thus the optimal balance between formalist and pragmatic or consequentialist adjudication is likely to depend on the particular context. Fundamentally, economists raise questions about the rationale of courts—not in a metaphysical but in a functional sense of their contribution to social welfare. At the microeconomic level this concerns the rationale for public rather than private adjudication (Cooter 1983). At the macroeconomic level, courts are seen among the mechanisms for adopting society's institutional framework to welfare-relevant changes (Hadfield 2008; La Porta et al. 2008). This suggests an impact of courts following different conventions of legal reasoning on social welfare (or its dynamic proxies such as growth or innovation). One may ask, for instance, whether the adaptation occurs differently in legal cultures which give judges discretion to consider social consequences in a forward-looking manner and adapt legal norms or in those where the canon of acceptable arguments binds judges more closely to rule-based reasoning.

3.4 CONCLUSION

Judicial reasoning is the paradigmatic case of legal reasoning and its jurisprudential analyses focus almost exclusively on adjudication. This overview followed suit and focused on economic considerations in and analyses of judicial interpretation of precedents and statutes.

As a sophisticated version of teleological reasoning, economics is a serious candidate to play a role *in* legal reasoning, providing (1) information about the likely consequences of alternative legal decisions, (2) instrumental arguments about the best means to achieve set goals, and (3) identifying desirable policy goals as background justifications for particular legal provisions, as part of purposive interpretation. This typically happens in contexts where statutes or legal precedents require or allow for "economic considerations" to motivate the decision or when standards of reasonableness require balancing competing principles and/or interests in broadly consequential terms.

Economic analyses *of* legal reasoning look at legal reasoning from an external perspective and either make explanatory contributions, for example by analyzing legal reasoning in public choice terms as a form of rational activity by legal officials, or address questions of institutional design of the following sort: what are the tasks that judges should be assigned to do, considering what they are able to do, given their motivations and system- and domain-specific constraints?

REFERENCES

Barnett, Randy. 1989. Foreword: Of Chickens and Eggs—The Compatibility of Moral Rights and Consequentialist Analyses. *Harvard Journal of Law and Public Policy* 12: 611–636.

Bell, John. 1995. Policy Arguments and Legal Reasoning. In *Informatics and the Foundations of Legal Reasoning*, ed. Zenon Bankowski, Ian White, and Ulrike Hahn, 73–97. Dordrecht: Kluwer.

Bix, Brian H. 2018. Introduction. In *Economic Approaches to Legal Reasoning and Interpretation*, ed. Brian H. Bix. Cheltenham: Elgar.

———. 2019. Law and Economics and the Role of Explanation: A Comment of Guido Calabresi, The Future of Law and Economics. *European Journal of Law and Economics* 48: 113–123.

Buchanan, James M. 1974. Good Economics, Bad Law. *Virginia Law Review* 60: 483–492.

Cane, Peter. 2000. Consequences in Judicial Reasoning. In *Oxford Essays in Jurisprudence*. Fourth Series, ed. Jeremy Horder, 41–59. Oxford: Oxford University Press.

Carbonell Bellolio, Flavia. 2011. Reasoning by Consequences: Applying Different Argumentation Structures to the Analysis of Consequentialist Reasoning in Judicial Decisions. *Cogency: Journal of Reasoning and Argumentation* 3: 81–104.

Coleman, Jules L. 1992. *Risks and Wrongs*. Cambridge: Cambridge University Press.

Cooter, Robert D. 1983. Objectives of Public and Private Judges. *Public Choice* 41: 107–132.

Cooter, Robert D., and Michael Gilbert. 2019. Constitutional Law and Economics. Forthcoming in *Research Methods in Constitutional Law: A Handbook*, ed. Malcolm Langford and David S. Law. Cheltenham: Elgar. Available at SSRN: https://ssrn.com/abstract=3123253

Cooter, Robert D., and Tom Ginsburg. 1996. Comparative Judicial Discretion: An Empirical Test of Economic Models. *International Review of Law and Economics* 16: 295–313.

Cooter, Robert D., and Daniel L. Rubinfeld. 1989. Economic Analysis of Legal Disputes and Their Resolution. *Journal of Economic Literature* 27: 1067–1097.

Craswell, Richard. 1993. Default Rules, Efficiency, and Prudence. *Southern California Interdisciplinary Law Journal* 3: 289–302.

Cserne, Péter. 2011. Consequence-Based Arguments in Legal Reasoning: A Jurisprudential Preface to Law and Economics. In *Efficiency, Sustainability, and Justice to Future Generations*, ed. Klaus Mathis, 31–54. Berlin and New York: Springer.

Dewatripont, Mathias, and Jean Tirole. 1999. Advocates. *Journal of Political Economy* 107: 1–39.

Dhami, Mandeep K. 2003. Psychological Models of Professional Decision Making. *Psychological Science* 14: 175–180.

Dietrich, Franz, and Christian List. 2013. A Reason-Based Theory of Rational Choice. *Noûs* 47: 104–134.

Dworkin, Ronald M. 1980. Is Wealth a Value? *Journal of Legal Studies* 9: 191–226.

Engel, Christoph. 2004. The Impact of Representation Norms on the Quality of Judicial Decisions. *MPI Collective Goods Preprints*, No. 2004/13. http://ssrn.com/abstract=617821

Epstein, Richard A. 1997. *Simple Rules for a Complex World*. Cambridge, MA: Harvard University Press.

Esposito, Fabrizio. 2020. Reverse Engineering Legal Reasoning. In *Economics in Legal Reasoning*, ed. Péter Cserne and Fabrizio Esposito, 139–154. London: Palgrave Macmillan.

Esposito, Fabrizio, and Giovanni Tuzet. 2019. Economic Consequences as Legal Values: A Legal Inferentialist Approach. In *Law and Economics as Interdisciplinary Exchange. Philosophical, Methodological and Historical Perspectives*, ed. Péter Cserne and Magdalena Małecka, 135–157. Abingdon: Routledge.

Farber, Daniel. 2000. Economic Efficiency and the Ex Ante Perspective. In *The Jurisprudential Foundations of Commercial and Corporate Law*, ed. Jody S. Kraus and Steven D. Walt, 54–86. Cambridge: Cambridge University Press.

Ferejohn, John A., and Barry R. Weingast. 1992. A Positive Theory of Statutory Interpretation. *International Review of Law and Economics* 12: 263–279.

Gigerenzer, Gerd, and Christoph Engel, eds. 2006. *Heuristics and the Law*. Boston: MIT Press.

Gould, John P. 1973. The Economics of Legal Conflicts. *Journal of Legal Studies* 2: 279–300.

Hadfield, Gillian J. 2008. The Levers of Legal Design: Institutional Determinants of the Quality of Law. *Journal of Comparative Economics* 36: 43–72.

Hubková, Pavlína. 2020. Economics in Judicial Decision-making: Four Types of Situations Where Judges May Apply Economics. In *Economics in Legal Reasoning*, ed. Péter Cserne and Fabrizio Esposito, 45–61. London: Palgrave Macmillan.

Kaplow, Louis, and Steven Shavell. 2002. *Fairness versus Welfare*. Cambridge, MA: Harvard University Press.

Katz, Avery Wiener. 2004. The Economics of Form and Substance in Contract Interpretation. *Columbia Law Review* 104: 496–538.

Klein, David E., and Gregory Mitchell, eds. 2010. *The Psychology of Judicial Decision Making*. Cambridge: Cambridge University Press.

Kornhauser, Lewis A. 1980. A Guide to the Perplexed Claims of Efficiency in the Law. *Hofstra Law Review* 8: 591–639.

———. 2017. The Economic Analysis of Law. *Stanford Encyclopedia of Philosophy* (Fall 2017 Edition). https://plato.stanford.edu/archives/fall2017/entries/legal-econanalysis/.

———. 2018a. Choosing Ends and Choosing Means: Teleological Reasoning in Law. In *Handbook of Legal Reasoning and Argumentation*, ed. Giorgio Bongiovanni et al., 387–412. New York: Springer.

———. 2018b. Economic Logic and Legal Logic. In *Handbook of Legal Reasoning and Argumentation*, ed. Giorgio Bongiovanni et al., 711–745. New York: Springer.

Kraus, Jody S. 2002. Philosophy of Contract Law. In *The Oxford Handbook of Jurisprudence and Philosophy of Law*, ed. Jules Coleman and Scott Shapiro, 687–751. Oxford: Oxford University Press.

La Porta, Rafael, Florencio Lopez-de-Silanes, and Andrei Shleifer. 2008. The Economic Consequences of Legal Origins. *Journal of Economic Literature* 46: 285–332.

Landes, William M. 1971. An Economic Analysis of the Courts. *Journal of Law and Economics* 14: 61–107.

Landes, William M., and Richard A. Posner. 1976. Legal Precedent: A Theoretical and Empirical Analysis. *Journal of Law and Economics* 19: 249–307.

Lieth, Oliver. 2007. *Die ökonomische Analyse des Rechts im Spiegelbild klassischer Argumentationsrestriktionen des Rechts und seiner Methodenlehre*. Baden-Baden: Nomos.

MacCormick, Neil. 1983. On Legal Decisions and Their Consequences: From Dewey to Dworkin. *New York University Law Review* 58: 239–258.

Petersen, Nils. 2017. *Proportionality and Judicial Activism. Fundamental Rights Adjudication in Canada, Germany and South Africa*. Cambridge: Cambridge University Press.

Pettit, Philip. 1991. Consequentialism. In *A Companion to Ethics*, ed. Peter Singer, 230–240. Oxford: Blackwell.

Portuese, Aurelien, Orla Gough, and Joseph Tanega. 2018. The Principle of Legal Certainty as a Principle of Economic Efficiency. *European Journal of Law and Economics* 44: 131–156.

Posner, Richard A. 1972. A Theory of Negligence. *Journal of Legal Studies* 1: 29–96.

———. 1973. An Economic Approach to Legal Procedure and Judicial Administration. *Journal of Legal Studies* 2: 399–458.

———. 1983. *The Economics of Justice*. 2nd ed. Chicago: University of Chicago Press.

———. 1987. The Constitution as an Economic Document. *George Washington Law Review* 56: 4–38.

———. 1990. *The Problems of Jurisprudence*. Cambridge, MA: Harvard University Press.

———. 1999. The Law and Economics of the Economic Expert Witness. *Journal of Economic Perspectives* 13: 91–99.

————. 2005. The Law and Economics of Contract Interpretation. *Texas Law Review* 83: 1581–1614.

————. 2007a. Tribute to Ronald Dworkin. And a Note on Pragmatic Adjudication. *New York University Annual Review of American Law* 63: 9–13.

————. 2007b. *Economic Analysis of Law*. 7th ed. New York: Aspen.

Priest, George L. 1977. The Common Law Process and the Selection of Efficient Rules. *Journal of Legal Studies* 6: 65–82.

Rubin, Paul H. 1977. Why Is the Common Law Efficient?. *Journal of Legal Studies* 6: 51–63.

————., ed. 2007. *The Evolution of Efficient Common Law*. Cheltenham: Elgar.

Rudden, Bernard. 1979. Consequences. *Juridical Review* 24: 193–201.

Schwartzstein, Linda A. 1994. An Austrian Economic View of the Legal Process. *Ohio State Law Journal* 55: 1009–1049.

Symposium. 1980. Efficiency as a Legal Concern. *Hofstra Law Review* 8: 485–770.

Teubner, Gunther, ed. 1995. *Entscheidungsfolgen als Rechtsgründe. Folgenorientiertes Argumentieren in rechtsvergleichender Sicht*. Baden-Baden: Nomos.

Tullock, Gordon. 1980. *Trials on Trial: The Pure Theory of Legal Procedure*. New York: Columbia University Press.

Westerman, Pauline. 2018. *Outsourcing the Law: A Philosophical Perspective on Regulation*. Cheltenham: Elgar.

White, Jefferson, and Dennis Patterson. 1999. *Introduction to Philosophy of Law*. Oxford: Oxford University Press.

PART II

Economics and Legal Interpretation

Economics in Judicial Decision-Making: Four Types of Situations Where Judges May Apply Economics

Pavlína Hubková

Abstract The chapter is based on the premise that economics may present epistemic difficulties for judges. It offers to conceptualize situations where judges may or have to apply economic thinking. The chapter focuses on four model categories where judges intentionally or unintentionally use economic considerations and economic arguments, or where there is a place for an economic consideration to be employed: issue of procedural economy and efficient management in everyday decision-making, abstract economic reasoning in explicitly economic fields of law, economic analysis of facts, and awareness of different economic theories that may have an impact on the judicial decision-making.

Keywords Judges • Procedural economy • Abstract economic reasoning • Economic analysis of facts • Economic theories

P. Hubková (✉)
Université du Luxembourg, Luxembourg, Luxemburg
e-mail: pavlina.hubkova@uni.lu

© The Author(s) 2020
P. Cserne, F. Esposito (eds.), *Economics in Legal Reasoning*,
Palgrave Studies in Institutions, Economics and Law,
https://doi.org/10.1007/978-3-030-40168-9_4

4.1   INTRODUCTION

Who is the legitimate owner of the foal? In a fairy tale, a wise and good king in a position of a judge had to resolve a dispute between a mare trader and a gelding trader. A little foal got lost and then it was found in the stable of the gelding trader. The mare trader claimed that the foal belonged to him. However, the king decided that because the foal was found in the stable of the gelding trader, the gelding trader must be its owner. A small boy commented on the decision saying that the king is not wise at all, because each and every kid in the kingdom knows that geldings cannot have foals. Was the king short of wisdom or intelligence? Probably not. He was just not familiar with the reproduction of horses and was led by a straightforward logic that foals belong where they are found. He was making a decision to settle the dispute in a situation that presented an epistemic difficulty for him. It might have been a matter of common sense for children in the kingdom, but in the eyes of the king, it was a completely unknown domain.

Nowadays, judges may face analogous epistemic difficulties when they adjudicate cases concerning a specific expertise or when they deal with a case belonging to a field where straightforward logic or seemingly common sense may lead to incorrect results. Cases pertaining to economic law, requiring economic expertise or including (complex) economic relations present a good example of situations where an average judge might feel lost or might not be aware of the lack of knowledge that might produce false conclusions.

It is certainly true that "judges are not economists. We do not expect to see in judges' opinions precise economic demonstrations of the kind found in a standard textbook. Judges do not derive a demand curve or a long-run supply curve" (Epstein 1996, p. 8). The role of judges does not include modeling economic reality or describing a detailed economic impact of a concrete decision. Nevertheless, there might be cases where it is very useful to understand the economic regularities, motives and incentives and (individual or general) consequences of possible solutions.

The aim of this chapter is to characterize model situations where judges have the opportunity to apply economics. It is presumed that knowledge of such model situations could help us to reveal possible epistemic difficulties that judges may encounter and to find ways to overcome them. The chapter focuses on four categories of situations that were intentionally chosen as model cases where the use of economics and economic considerations differs by the level of abstraction, by the level of complexity and by the kind of immediate consequences of a decision based on such considerations. The first category (abstract economics in legal reasoning) deals with the understanding of abstract economic scenarios and their translation into law. The second category encompasses situations where judges have to apply economic thinking on facts of a given case and, in a certain way, decide as if they were economic experts. The third category deals with economic theories and their diverse consequences on decision-making. These three categories present different types of economics in judicial reasoning, while the final fourth category is about the economics of judicial decision-making. It covers economic considerations of a judge as a rational agent in her/his daily decision-making on procedural aspects and time management. The examples in the chapter come from EU law and especially economic aspects of EU law and competition law, Czech administrative law and Czech civil law. However, it is presumed that these uses of economics appear in other legal systems and other legal domains as well.

4.2   ABSTRACT ECONOMICS IN LEGAL REASONING OF JUDGES

The first category of economics in judicial decision-making covers the application of abstract economic reasoning as a specific type of legal reasoning. In other words, we can call it economically informed legal reasoning.[1] This category is based on the assumption that legal reasoning and economic reasoning do not stand in opposition. Rather, economic reasoning means a type of legal reasoning that takes economic arguments into consideration. It represents a way of economic thinking within law. It must be highlighted that such economic reasoning does not equal reasoning with models or hard data, using solely quantitative arguments based on calculations, graphs or abstract models. The specificity of economic reasoning lies in the choice of acceptable arguments and in the way they are evaluated and linked according to their economic relevance.

Economic reasoning of judges is a part of the "process of justification" (MacCormick 1978, p. 5). In other words, economic thinking is employed to make an economically informed justification of a judicial decision.

---

[1] On legal reasoning, see Canale and Tuzet (2020). On economics in legal reasoning, see Cserne (2020).

Within the process of economically informed justification, the reality of a given case or of a model situation is seen through a grid of economic relevance: From among all aspects and features of a (concrete or abstract) case, we have to choose factors that are relevant from an economic point of view (factors related to rational decision-making on the use of scarce resources) and then identify the economic causality between them. In the end, the justification arises from the mutual relations of the chosen factors.

Let us take an example of the reasoning of the Court of Justice of the European Union (CJEU) in the field of competition law. In the following definition of the abuse of dominance through exclusivity rebates we can see an economic argument: "Where an undertaking in a dominant position directly or indirectly ties its customers by an exclusive supply obligation, that constitutes an abuse since it deprives the customer of the ability to choose his sources of supply and denies other producers access to the market."[2] The reality of a business practice based on fidelity rebates is composed by different aspects. The CJEU chooses among them and focuses on the *nature* of exclusivity clauses (customers have a duty to buy a certain product from the dominant supplier; such a duty may be both direct and indirect), the *direct impact* of the exclusivity clauses on customers (customers have a duty to purchase only from the dominant supplier, therefore they are not allowed to start purchasing from another supplier) and the *secondary impact* on competitors/potential suppliers (if a substantial number of customers are tied by the exclusivity obligation, there is almost no market left for actual or potential competitors to offer their goods; therefore actual competitors are forced to leave the market, and potential competitors are prevented from entering the market). All these factors are connected by a causal link: when a substantial proportion of customers is tied by exclusivity clauses, they may not purchase from alternative producers who are consequently forced to leave the market, and as a result the competition is weakened. Such a scenario is complemented by a normative claim: since exclusivity rebates provided by a dominant undertaking lead, in the very end, to lessening competition on the market, such a business practice is against the goal of preserving undistorted competition, and therefore it should be deemed abusive in the sense of Article 102 TFEU.

---

[2] Judgment of the Court of First Instance, T-83/91, Tetra Pak v. Commission, ECLI:EU:T:1994:246, para 137.

Explained in this manner, this scenario reveals a complex economic argument with normative content. Nevertheless, economic arguments may also appear in a simple way where a cause and a consequence, or a motive and a consequence, are logically linked. Abstract economic arguments may explain behavior or motives for a certain behavior. In competition law, the explanation may regard the motive of the dominant undertaking/cartelist, the consequential behavior of actual or potential competitors, or even the behavior of customers and consumers.

For example, an argument used in predatory pricing cases is based on the economic premise that the behavior of an economically rational entrepreneur is driven by the aim to maximize profits. Therefore, a dominant undertaking would not intentionally suffer loss without a plan to recover it in the future. The CJEU explains why an undertaking would pursue pricing below average variable costs in the following sentence: "In such a case, there is no conceivable economic purpose other than the elimination of a competitor, since each item produced and sold entails a loss for the undertaking."[3]

In this case,[4] we can see how judges articulate economically informed arguments; that is in order to underpin their decisions, they use reasons that are based on economically relevant causal links. Implementing such aspects of economic knowledge into legal reasoning may be considered as "an intermediate step in a legal decision" (Sibony 2012, p. 42) and it is an example of a situation where economics becomes an intrinsic part of legal reasoning.

4.3   ECONOMIC ANALYSIS OF FACTS

The second category covers the economic analysis of facts in a given case. In contrast to the previous category, it relates to economic considerations of a particular behavior, its real consequences and decisions on economically sound remedies. Economic thinking within this category comes closer to the activity of economic experts.[5] A good example of this type of economic thinking can be found in the field of private enforcement of competition law, especially in the decisions on the amount of damages.

---

[3] Judgment of the Court of First Instance, T-340/03, France Télécom v. Commission, ECLI:EU:T:2007:22, para 224.
[4] More examples in Hubková (2014).
[5] See Broulík (2020) and Giocoli (2020).

The quantification of competition damages is predominantly based on the analysis of a hypothetical situation which never happened but which would have surely or almost surely have happened without the breach of competition law. Creating such a hypothetical scenario requires not only economic knowledge but also an ability to assess the given facts and apply those data that are relevant and that show trustworthily how the market could have developed and how exactly the injured party was harmed. Normally, the modeling of a hypothetical scenario and the quantification of a particular harm would be tasks for an economic expert. However, EU Directive 2014/104/EU (Article 17) foresees that there may be situations where it is practically impossible or excessively difficult for the claimant to quantify precisely the harm suffered just on the basis of the evidence available, and in such a case, it empowers the national courts with the competence to estimate the extent of harm.

The estimation takes place if and only if it is proved that the claimant really suffered harm (the claimant complies with the burden of proof) but it is objectively impossible or excessively difficult to prove the actual extent of harm. In such a case, the judge may not decide just upon a free consideration or limitless discretion. On the contrary, the judge must take into consideration all circumstances of a given case that enable a conclusion regarding the quantitative aspects of the extent of harm. The judge may apply indirect indices or must be, at least, able to justify her/his limits of discretion and to explain which circumstances lead to the determination of those limits.[6]

When estimating the harm, the judge has to be inevitably familiar with the basics of microeconomics. She/he has to know the basic rules of interaction between supply and demand, the concept of elasticity, the mechanism behind how the market price is determined, the relation between price effects and volume effects and so on.[7] Similarly, estimation

---

[6] The determination of detailed rules on how the courts should estimate damages is left to national law (Recital 46 of the Directive). In Czech law, see the judgment of the Supreme Court, 21 December 2009, no. 30 Cdo 5188/2007 or the judgment of the High Court in Prague, 17 January 2012, no. 4 Cmo 29/2011-252.

[7] Communication from the Commission on quantifying harm in actions for damages based on breaches of Article 101 or 102 of the Treaty on the Functioning of the European Union (Text with EEA relevance) (2013/C 167/07), p. 3.

by the judge occurs when a passing-on defense is raised by the defendant. The defendant may claim that the cartel overcharge was passed by the claimant on her/his own customers, and therefore the actual harm suffered by the claimant is less extensive. The Directive explicitly (Article 12) empowers the courts to estimate the amount of overcharge that has been passed on further in the distribution channel.

The European Commission has recently published guidelines for national courts on how to estimate the amount of passing on.[8] The document is highly technical and requires that judges apply not only common sense but also thorough knowledge of microeconomics. The judge must understand which factors may have influence on the share of overcharge that can be passed on to indirect purchasers: demand elasticity, the market power of the direct purchaser, the market power of other market players, the type of costs influenced by overcharge, the share of input influenced by overcharge, the overall value of products, vertical integration of direct and indirect purchasers and so on.

When estimating the share of passing on, the judge has to estimate three aspects: overcharge, price effects and volume effects. Each of these three aspects requires different data and different methodologies (Durand and Williams 2017). It is up to the judge to determine the share of passing on as precisely as possible and to take into consideration all available data.[9] Even in situations where quantification of damages will be delivered by an economic expert,[10] it is an obligation of the judge to assess the quality of the expert report[11]—mainly in cases where both parties submit different and naturally contradictory reports.

The field of competition damages and the task to estimate the extent of damage therefore present an interesting legal sphere where it is important for judges to understand and apply at least basic economic principles.

---

[8] Communication from the Commission. Guidelines for national courts on how to estimate the share of overcharge which was passed on to the indirect purchaser (2019/C 267/07).

[9] Similarly, in the field of tax law, see the judgment of the CJEU, C-147/01, Weber's Wine World and Others, EU:C:2003:533, paras 96 and 100.

[10] See Broulík (2020).

[11] See, for example, a judgment of the UK court: The High Court of Justice. Queen's Bench Division. BSkyB v. EDS, [2010] EWHC 86 (TCC) (26/01/2010), para 303.

4.4   AWARENESS OF THE EXISTENCE OF DIFFERENT ECONOMIC THEORIES

In the third category of economic thinking within adjudication, we leave the ground of practical economic tools and take off toward the clouds of competing economic theories. This category covers awareness of the fact that there might be different economic theories and that their application might lead to diverse results.[12] Within this category, the economic argument could be considered close to or even overlapping with a political argument. The awareness of this layer of economic knowledge could be useful for judges in order to understand, at least, the political and economic context of their decision-making. Ideally, judges should know that economic arguments are not always value-neutral. This category of economic thinking does not include any specific tools to be used by judges in deciding individual cases, but it offers a broader look at the implications of their decision-making.[13]

Presumably, we might find differences in legal reasoning and legal outputs of judges according to the chosen economic theory. The approach advocated by mainstream neoclassical economics may lead to different results than approaches supported by various streams of alternative schools of economic thought, such as post-Keynesianism, institutional economics, feminist economics, social economics, Marxist economics, endogenous growth theory and so on (Beker 2019; Reinert et al. 2016; Lawson 2006). We might find a good example of this in the clash between fundamental economic freedoms and social goals in the case law of the CJEU. The following text does not necessarily criticize the approach taken by the CJEU; nor does it suggest that judges should deviate from settled case law. It rather points out that the legal approach held by the CJEU is not determined by an inevitable and value-neutral economic logic but follows one of economic theories that became, at a certain time, predominant.

When judges have to balance economic freedoms and social goals, their choice of a particular economic theory will presumably influence the balancing process as such, and, accordingly, also the final decision (Kaupa 2013, p. 65). European integration was considered, since the very

---

[12] See Giocoli (2020).

[13] It is important to note that the previous two categories of use of economics are typically influenced by a leading economic theory. Even the experts hired by opposing parties usually subscribe to the same theory and they disagree on how it applies to the facts.

beginning, an economic project. Many rules contained in the Treaties are therefore based on certain economic ideas but the economic theories behind such ideas were never explicitly proclaimed.[14] The fundamental economic freedoms, as the cornerstone of the internal market, may thus be interpreted and analyzed through different economic lenses. The choice of the lenses would probably influence one's perception of the goal of a given rule and of the outcome of a particular decision.

The standard balancing formula in EU law is the "internal market proportionality test" that compares a market freedom (individual economic right) on the one hand as the rule with the regulation in public interest (restriction of the individual economic right justified by the public interest objective) on the other hand as the exception. The leading principle of market freedoms is based on a (mainstream economics, neoclassical) presumption (Mulder 2018) that free movement of factors of production leads to allocative efficiency (Samuelson 1948), which means an "allocation of resources in which value is maximized" (Posner 2007, p. 11), and that it inevitably helps economic growth which is the desired goal of society.[15]

This mainstream neoclassical approach is rather taken for granted and not questioned in CJEU case law. A good example may be seen in the Viking case (C-438/05). The competing values in this case were freedom of establishment as a market freedom on one side and collective action of workers as a social value (fundamental right) on the other side. Concerning the facts, Viking Line was a Finnish shipping company that provided ferry services from Finland to Estonia. In order to decrease costs, the company decided to replace the Finnish flag of its ship by an Estonian flag, which would allow the payment of lower wages according to Estonian law. The Finnish labor union (supported by the Estonian labor union) started a collective action in order to prevent the relocation.

The CJEU acknowledged the right to take collective action as a "fundamental right which forms an integral part of the general principles of [EU] law", but added that "the exercise of that right may none the less be subject to certain restrictions".[16] In the next step, the CJEU argued that

---

[14] Arguably, the process of European integration was influenced significantly by ordoliberalism. See, for example, Nedergaard (2013).

[15] See article 3(3) TEU that stipulates that the EU "shall work for the sustainable development of Europe based on *balanced economic growth and price stability*" (emphasis added).

[16] Judgment of the Court of Justice, C-438/05, Viking Line, ECLI:EU:C:2007:772, para 44.

the collective action represents a restriction to the freedom of establishment as it "has the effect of making less attractive, or even pointless [...] Viking's exercise of its freedom of establishment, because it prevents Viking [...] from enjoying the same treatment in the host Member State as other economic operators established in that State".[17] Then it acknowledged that although the protection of workers is a legitimate interest that may justify restricting fundamental freedom, this may only take place if it were established that the jobs or conditions of employment of the members of the trade union employed by Viking Line were genuinely jeopardized or under serious threat, and if the particular collection action was suitable to ensure the achievement of the objectives pursued and did not go beyond what is necessary to attain that objective.[18]

The approach of the CJEU has been criticized as being based on a "peculiar understanding of economic freedoms" that gives priority "to the rights of capital holders over the socio-economic rights" (Menéndez 2011, p. 168). Arguably, the peculiarity lies in adopting the neoclassical understanding of the market economy. The neoclassical aspect of reasoning of the CJEU lies at the core of the traditional internal market balancing formula: free movement leads to allocative efficiency, and therefore inevitably brings about positive outcomes for the whole society—it is the rule (Brisimi 2016, p. 62). Any competing fundamental values may prevail only as an exception if they are justified and proportionate. In other words, the economic freedoms are considered a motor of integration while the socio-economic rights seem to appear as somehow tolerated brakes.

A risk that arises from such an approach could be that the internal market and its core principles are considered a nonpolitical structure (Bugaric 2013, p. 12) and as a value-neutral system that is unavoidable for economic growth and the well-being of society. However, such an understanding of the internal market is the consequence of a highly political choice from among diverse economic theories. If an alternative economic theory were chosen, the balancing exercise could be different.

For example, post-Keynesian economics would not see the free movement of companies as flawless and always economically advantageous. It might be dangerous when it "allows companies to pursue rent-seeking behaviour by playing off different regions and different labour forces against each other" (Kaupa 2013, p. 67). From the post-Keynesian point

---

[17] Ibid., para 72.
[18] Ibid., para 90.

of view that focuses more on the demand-side of the market, the way resources are distributed among individuals has a more significant impact on economic growth than the efficiency of production (Lavoie 2011, p. 11). If this theory were applied in case of a clash between fundamental economic freedoms and socioeconomic rights, the latter would not lose so easily.

Endogenous growth theory would not support the standard balancing formula either. According to this theory, economic growth has endogenous, rather than exogenous, causes. The growth is a result of investment in innovation, knowledge and human capital (Aghion and Howitt 1997). From the perspective of this theory, a danger is seen in the fact that from a strictly neoclassical approach, countries with the comparative advantage in lower wages would not be motivated to technically more demanding production and would get stuck in low-tech and less productive industries. This would lead to asymmetry in the economic growth between respective countries.

The question remains how such alternative approaches could be translated into judicial reasoning. A potential way could be to use the Schmidberger type of double proportionality test[19] where both competing fundamental values stand on an equal footing (Lenaerts 2012, p. 393). In such a case, the justification in favor of socioeconomic rights could lie in "possible positive long term effects of industrial action for the interests of workers" (Hős 2010, p. 246).

Anyway, these examples show that different economic theories underpinning a certain legal interpretation lead to different results. Therefore, when deciding hard cases where competing fundamental values must be balanced, judges should at least bear in mind that the balancing exercise as such is not value-neutral. The very construction of a balancing formula and the entry value of each of the competing interests may influence the outcome. The conventional internal market proportionality test is based on neoclassical assumptions, but judges should know that there are alternative economic approaches and that market freedoms may be subject to various ways of economic interpretation.

For judges, the knowledge of different economic theories represents "bonus knowledge". It might be useful mainly for higher court judges who contribute, while interpreting the law, to contouring policies.

[19] Judgment of the Court of Justice, C-112/00, Schmidberger v. Austria, ECLI:EU:C: 2003:333, paras 78–79.

Economic ideas and assumptions influence policy choices that are consequently incorporated into legal rules and may have an impact on how these rules are interpreted.

4.5   EFFICIENT CASE MANAGEMENT AND PROCEDURAL ECONOMY

The fourth category of judges' economic thinking embraces economic considerations related to the management of workload, the consequences of procedural decisions and procedural economy in general. While planning hearings, taking evidence, appointing experts, scheduling, joining cases together, deciding to stay the proceedings, making breaks in working on one case and so on, judges have the opportunity to think "economically" and balance costs and benefits.

A judge, as any economically rational agent, has to make various decisions in order to work efficiently. Within the framework of the judicial decision-making, efficiency[20] could be concretized and translated as the optimal balance between, on the one hand, legal accuracy and fairness of the decision and, on the other hand, the aim to deliver the decision in a reasonable time frame and to avoid excessive costs (Krajewski 2019, pp. 222–223).

As an example, let us look at the decision-making of a judge in a civil procedure.[21] She/he must perform a balancing exercise in situations where she/he decides upon procedural steps. For example, scheduling an extra hearing where additional evidence is taken might lead to a more precise fact finding, but it takes up time which could be dedicated to another case. On the other hand, when the first-instance judge is satisfied with the already given facts and denies taking other evidence, the court of appeals may conclude that fact finding was not complete and thus cancel the decision and return it to the first-instance judge who has to work on the same case again.[22] As the interactions with higher courts represent repeated games, after some time and with increasing experience, judges may,

---

[20] On the basic economic model of the legal process, see Cserne (2020, pp. 35–37).

[21] The examples are taken from Czech law, but they may appear in other jurisdictions as well.

[22] Article 219a and article 221 of the Act no. 99/1963 Sb., Czech Civil procedural code.

presumably, estimate whether, in a given case, it is worth bearing a risk or whether it is safer to spend more time on the case.

Within proceedings of a particular case, the judge has to bear in mind procedural economy that requires costs of proceedings to be as low as possible, but not to jeopardize the objective of the procedure. The aim of the principle is to make the proceedings simple and brief and to avoid unnecessary steps and excessive costs (Grubbs 2003, p. 24). Rules on procedural economy may be embedded already in codes of procedure, but there might be situations where judges are, within their own limits of discretion, free to make their own procedural decisions based on their own cost–benefit analysis of a given situation. For example, a judge may, for the purposes of procedural economy, join cases pending before her/him that are similar in facts or that involve the same parties.[23]

There might be situations where a judge decides whether to stay proceedings or not. Let us consider a Czech civil procedure on competition damages. If the administrative proceedings of the competition authority that would lead to an outcome that might be decisive for a civil case are in progress, the judge might decide to stay civil proceedings and wait for the administrative decision.[24] However, when it is apparent that the administrative proceedings will be too lengthy, it might seem more efficient to decide the administrative action on her/his own.[25] However, there is a risk that if the final administrative decision is contrary to the initial judicial decision, the judicial proceedings will have to be renewed, which incurs additional work for the judge and additional costs for the parties. In both situations, a judge has to evaluate whether the case is so complex that it is better to wait for the administrative decision, or whether it would delay the exercise of justice excessively.[26]

Moreover, economic thinking of a rational agent may be found even in banal situations when judges consider the efficiency of their own working habits. For example, a judge might decide whether to take a break from

---

[23] Article 112 of the Act no. 99/1963 Sb., Czech Civil procedural code.
[24] Article 109(2)(c) of the Act no. 99/1963 Sb., Czech Civil procedural code.
[25] Article 135(2) of the Act no. 99/1963 Sb., Czech Civil procedural code.
[26] In general, Czech courts are not very keen to stay proceedings on competition damages. For example, in case no 15 Cm 56/2012, the Municipal Court in Prague (first-instance court) stayed proceedings in order to wait for the decision of the competition authority, but the High Court in Prague (appeal court) dismissed this decision saying that it would delay the exercise of justice excessively (case no Cmo 126/2013-437) and ordered the first-instance court to continue.

working on one case and start working on another case in order to feel refreshed, with the aim of returning to the first case later, or whether it is more efficient to finish the first case at one go, because there is a risk that after some time she/he may forget some important aspects of the case and will have to study the case from the very beginning again. Working on several cases at the same time might keep the judge refreshed, but when there are too many open cases, it might lead to overall inefficiency (Coviello et al. 2014).

In the latter example, we can see that a simplified version of the cost–benefit analysis is part of the daily decision-making of any judge. Even if judges are not fully aware of their own economic thinking, they may employ economic considerations very often. While it is interesting to keep such situations in mind, the examples might open a fruitful field of empirical studies on the efficiency of (civil) justice (Palumbo et al. 2013; Epstein and Knight 2017) or the efficiency of the judicial system (Voigt 2016).

4.6   Conclusion

This chapter mentioned four different model situations in which judges may face economics or may apply economic arguments. When deciding a case that belongs to an explicit economic area of law, judges must master economic reasoning and understand economic causal links between various aspects of a certain behavior, its motives and consequences, together with the overall impact of such a behavior on markets and the economy. When judges are tasked with estimating competition damages, they must carefully assess all given facts, understand economic theory on how damages occur and determine reasonably the probable extent of damage. In a situation where judges compare competing fundamental values, they must be aware that the balancing exercise as such is not value-neutral, and that the construction of a legal (proportionality) test might be influenced by a particular economic theory. Finally, in their everyday work, judges must balance costs and benefits of their discretionary steps.

Knowledge of at least some basic economics may be helpful to any judge at any instance. For judges who deal with cases within explicitly economic fields, it is important to understand the economic assumptions behind these legal domains more profoundly and to be able to apply even complex economic arguments. The awareness of a leading economic theory that shapes case law could help judges to understand the overall context of their decision-making. A rigorous and transparent work with economic considerations could enhance the quality of decision-making and it could even increase legal certainty. Our knowledge of different situations where economics may be applied could hopefully help us to assess the quality of the courts' outputs. Once we know which situations require which form of economic thinking, we may better assess whether the approach taken by the judge in a particular case was right and fair.

Potentially, knowing different scenarios where economics may play a role could be useful when thinking about the proper (economic) education for judges. No judge wants to look stupid and undereducated—even in the field of economics. In order to avoid mocking by each and every kid in the kingdom, all judges should rather study at least some basics of economics. It is, nonetheless, another story.

REFERENCES

Aghion, Philippe, and Peter W. Howitt. 1997. *Endogenous Growth Theory.* Cambridge, MA: The MIT Press.

Beker, Víctor A., ed. 2019. *Alternative Approaches to Economic Theory: Complexity, Post Keynesian and Ecological Economics.* Routledge Frontiers of Political Economy. New York: Routledge.

Brisimi, Vasiliki S. 2016. *The Interface between Competition and the Internal Market: Market Separation under Article 102 TFEU.* Oxford: Hart Publishing.

Broulík, Jan. 2020. What is Forensic Economics? In *Economics in Legal Reasoning*, ed. Péter Cserne and Fabrizio Esposito, 83–99. London: Palgrave Macmillan.

Bugaric, Bojan. 2013. Europe Against the Left? On Legal Limits to Progressive Politics. *LSE "Europe in Question" Discussion Paper Series*, No. 61.

Canale, Damiano, and Giovanni Tuzet. 2020. What is Legal Reasoning About: A Jurisprudential Perspective. In *Economics in Legal Reasoning*, ed. Péter Cserne and Fabrizio Esposito, 9–24. London: Palgrave Macmillan.

Coviello, Decio, Andrea Ichino, and Nicola Persico. 2014. Time Allocation and Task Juggling. *American Economic Review* 104 (2): 609–623. https://doi.org/10.1257/aer.104.2.609.

Cserne, Péter. 2020. Economic Approaches to Legal Reasoning: An Overview. In *Economics in Legal Reasoning*, ed. Péter Cserne and Fabrizio Esposito, 25–41. London: Palgrave Macmillan.

Durand, Benoît, and Iestyn Williams. 2017. The Importance of Accounting for Passing-on When Calculating Damages That Result from Infringement of Competition Law. *ERA Forum* 18 (1): 79–94. https://doi.org/10.1007/s12027-017-0458-3.

Epstein, Lee, and Jack Knight. 2017. The Economic Analysis of Judicial Behavior. In *The Oxford Handbook of U.S. Judicial Behavior*, ed. Lee Epstein and Stefanie A. Lindquist. Oxford: Oxford University Press.

Epstein, Richard Allen. 1996. *Economics and the Judges. The Case for Simple Rules and Boring Courts.* New Zealand Business Roundtable.

Giocoli, Nicola. 2020. Why US Judges Reject Economic Experts? In *Economics in Legal Reasoning*, ed. Péter Cserne and Fabrizio Esposito, 101–117. London: Palgrave Macmillan.

Grubbs, Shelby R. 2003. *International Civil Procedure.* WLGS 5. The Hague: Kluwer Law International.

Hős, Nikolett. 2010. The Principle of Proportionality in Viking and Laval: An Appropriate Standard of Judicial Review? *European Labour Law Journal* 1 (2): 236–253. https://doi.org/10.1177/201395251000100204.

Hubková, Pavlína. 2014. Economic Reasoning in the Court of Justice of the EU: A Study on the Use of Economics in Competition Case-Law. EUI LLM thesis. http://hdl.handle.net/1814/34406

Kaupa, Clemens. 2013. Maybe Not Activist Enough? On the Court's Alleged Neoliberal Bias in Its Recent Labor Cases. In *Judicial Activism at the European Court of Justice*, ed. Mark Dawson, Bruno de Witte, and Elise Muir, 56–75. Cheltenham, UK: Edward Elgar Publishing Limited.

Krajewski, Michał. 2019. The Many-Faced Court: The Value of Participation in Annulment Proceedings. *European Constitutional Law Review* 15 (2): 220–246. https://doi.org/10.1017/S157401961900018X.

Lavoie, Marc. 2011. History and Methods of Post-Keynesian Economics. In *A Modern Guide to Keynesian Macroeconomics and Economic Policies*, ed. Eckhard Hein and Engelbert Stockhammer. Cheltenham: Edward Elgar.

Lawson, Tony. 2006. The Nature of Heterodox Economics. *Cambridge Journal of Economics* 30 (4): 483–505. https://doi.org/10.1093/cje/bei093.

Lenaerts, Koen. 2012. Exploring the Limits of the EU Charter of Fundamental Rights. *European Constitutional Law Review* 8 (3): 375–403. https://doi.org/10.1017/S1574019612000260.

MacCormick, Neil. 1978. *Legal Reasoning and Legal Theory.* Clarendon Law Series. Oxford [Eng.]; New York: Clarendon Press; Oxford University Press.

Menéndez, Agustín José. 2011. A Proportionate Constitution? Economic Freedoms, Substantive Constitutional Choices and Dérapages in European Union Law. In *Hope, Reluctance or Fear? The Democratic Consequences of the Case Law of the European Court of Justice*, ed. Flavia Carbonell, Agustín José Menéndez, and John Erik Fossum, 167–252. Oslo: ARENA Centre for European Studies.

Mulder, Jotte. 2018. Unity and Diversity in the European Union's Internal Market Case Law: Towards Unity in 'Good Governance'? *Utrecht Journal of*

International and European Law 34 (1): 4–23. https://doi.org/10.5334/ujiel.454.

Nedergaard, Peter. 2013. The Influence of Ordoliberalism in European Integration Processes—A Framework for Ideational Influence with Competition Policy and the Economic and Monetary Policy as Examples. *MPRA Paper*, No. 52331. https://mpra.ub.uni-muenchen.de/52331/

Palumbo, Giuliana, Giulia Giupponi, Luca Nunziata, and Juan S. Mora-Sanguinetti. 2013. The Economics of Civil Justice: New Cross-Country Data and Empirics. *OECD Economics Department Working Papers 1060*. https://doi.org/10.1787/5k41w04ds6kf-en

Posner, Richard A. 2007. *Economic Analysis of Law*. 7th ed. New York: Aspen.

Reinert, Erik S., Jayati Ghosh, and Rainer Kattel, eds. 2016. *Handbook of Alternative Theories of Economic Development*. Cheltenham, UK and Northampton, MA: Edward Elgar Publishing.

Samuelson, Paul A. 1948. International Trade and the Equalisation of Factor Prices. *The Economic Journal* 58 (230): 163. https://doi.org/10.2307/2225933.

Sibony, Anne-Lise. 2012. Limits of Imports from Economics into Competition Law. In *The Global Limits of Competition Law*, ed. Ioannis Lianos and Daniel D. Sokol, 39–53. Stanford: Stanford Law Books.

Voigt, Stefan. 2016. Determinants of Judicial Efficiency: A Survey. *European Journal of Law and Economics* 42: 183–208.

CHAPTER 5

Characterizing Economic and Legal Approaches to the Regulation of Market Interactions

Fernando Gómez Pomar

Abstract This chapter provides an overview of how EU private law (and national European private laws) and, more specifically, contract and consumer law do not see eye to eye with economic—and law and economics—views over those kinds of interactions. With some illustrations from ECJ case law as motivating the study, it is argued that the divergent approaches reflect a deep divide between the intellectual goals and perspectives in both disciplines. This is to be lamented, since a greater openness by legal theory and legal academics toward economic ways of looking at market interactions would greatly enrich and refine the functioning of legal systems.

Keywords Law and economics • Legal perspective on economic interactions • Influence of economic theory and empirics

F. Gómez Pomar (✉)
Universitat Pompeu Fabra, Barcelona, Spain
e-mail: fernando.gomez@upf.edu

© The Author(s) 2020
P. Cserne, F. Esposito (eds.), *Economics in Legal Reasoning*,
Palgrave Studies in Institutions, Economics and Law,
https://doi.org/10.1007/978-3-030-40168-9_5

63

5.1   INTRODUCTION

The way in which legal notions are conceived, legal modes of thinking work, and the elements or inputs to be brought into them, influence the areas—in contemporary societies and legal systems, a large number—governed by legal rules, both in terms of determining legal outcomes and making sense of the legal solutions.

Economics as an intellectual field has experienced significant changes in the past decades. Economic theory and economic methods have greatly expanded their scope of application to cover many dimensions in the workings of societies but, more importantly for present purposes, their sophistication, realism and accuracy have increased substantially in terms of explaining the functioning and effects of economic interactions.

Game theory and information economics, empirical techniques with more structured data analysis and inference allowing more rigorous causal claims, statistical treatment of big data and behavioral analysis have joined forces in substantially transforming, and expanding, the economic understanding of how transactions and markets work.

To be honest, legal thinking has not played any meaningful role in the recent evolution of economics, not even in the (multiple) areas of common interest, although the attention paid by economists to institutional matters (including the workings of legal systems) and the recognition of their importance have substantially increased in recent years.

When one looks at the legal world, despite the radical transformation of economics and its output (both in terms of substantive knowledge and of methods), the law, legal thinking and legal practice are broadly immune to economic inputs and influence. Even legal domains directly interested in how firms interact with other firms and with consumers through contracting and markets remain, with a few exceptions—both geographical and disciplinary—largely unconcerned by those developments in economics, and by economic insights more generally. More specifically, if one thinks of the receptiveness of courts and legal scholarship, at least in the European[1] context, toward developments in economics (and law and economics), connected with game theory, information economics, econometrics and

[1] The European experience, perhaps similar to that of other legal contexts (Latin America, among others), differs from that of the US, although the true influence of Law and Economics there is a matter of debate: Garoupa and Ulen (2008, p. 1555).

empirical methods,[2] the emerging picture is one that can be characterized as cold, when not hostile (Alemanno and Sibony 2015, p. 22).

In contrast, behavioral analyses, including behavioral economics and law and economics, and specifically their fundamental approach, findings and implications for policy in various areas of interest for lawmaking and legal regulation, have been received with a warm glow by a substantial, attentive group of scholars within the European legal academia.[3] Whether this has had a deeper impact upon mainstream European legal scholarship, even the one dealing with consumer contracting, let alone on courts and legal practice, is a different matter. In fact, I fear that one should remain skeptical as to how seriously behavioral concerns, insights and, above all, modes of thinking about interactions and the role of regulatory interventions are truly making significant advances into the operations of consumer law in Europe. As has been recently observed, the Court of Justice of the European Union (the CJEU) shows a clear reluctance to explicitly refer to economic arguments (Franck 2017, p. 110).

To economically minded scholars, why, when dealing with legal dimensions of economic interactions, law and legal scholarship in Europe exhibits an ostensible disregard *vis-à-vis* economic insights appears puzzling and worthy of an attempted explanation. To be sure, economics as an academic discipline remains largely ignorant of the actual workings of the law, and tends to disregard the contributions from legal scholarship illuminating the legal and institutional foundations of societies and economies (Garoupa 2012). Even Ronald Coase (1988, pp. 158–159 and following), the father of law and economics, complained about this, and argued that it weakened the real-world appeal of economic contributions. One could even question the pretense of economics (or of some economists, at least) to dictate methods and policy advice in other areas of social science without a deeper knowledge of the subtleties and the complicated workings of those areas.[4] The law may be a prototypical example of this failed imperial expansionist campaign into a very complex area of human and social experience.

---

[2] For instance, a recent special issue on "Empirical Methods for the Law" was published in a European economic journal (*Journal of Institutional and Theoretical Economics*, vol. 174, 2018), and very few contributions were authored by European legal scholars.

[3] See Micklitz et al. (2018), Mathis and Tor (2016) and Alemanno and Sibony (2015).

[4] Coase (1994, p. 42), ironically, characterized this attitude with an apt historical metaphor: "At a time when the King of England claimed to be also King of France he was not always welcome in Paris".

The potential deficiencies of the economic ventures into other intellectual fields are surely relevant, but not my intended focus. I am more interested in the workings of legal systems and in how the intellectual views and tools used by courts and legal academics affect the way in which the machinery of the law influences social and economic outcomes. Thus, I will leave for others (recently, Calabresi 2016, p. 2 and following) the "economic" side of the divide or fault between economics and law.

The goal of the chapter is to present the argument that, in addition to other factors, the "essentials" of legal approaches to behavior in general make it hard for legal thinking to be receptive to economic perspectives about market behavior. Thus, legal institutions—courts, most notably—and legal scholarship are reluctant to familiarize themselves, to consider, let alone to share and use the "essentials" of economic analyses—theoretical and empirical, behavioral and nonbehavioral—that try to explain actions and choices by participants in economic interactions. The distinctive "legal" approach (as markedly contrasting with the economic) plays a large role in the perceived self-sufficiency of legal thinking about market behavior that underlies the still dominant views in European case law and literature.

5.2   Some Landmark EU Consumer Contract Cases Showing a Clear Disregard for Economic Thinking

In this section, I present a brief sample of CJEU cases turning the back toward economic input. These cases, however, provide a clear illustration about the fact that the most influential court in consumer law in Europe, when confronted by interpretive conundrums on consumer contracts, utterly disregards economic input (theoretical and empirical; behavioral and nonbehavioral alike). I want to emphasize that in these cases I do not have an issue with the disposition of the case as such by the CJEU, but with the "legalistic" approach by the Court.

A very compelling example, I believe, is *Matei*.[5] The decision by the Court concerned whether a 'risk charge' applied by a bank in the contract with the borrowers would qualify or not as an unfair term in a consumer credit contract. Specifically, the controversial issue was the application or not to the 'risk charge' of the "core term" exception of the unfairness test under art. 4 (2) of the Unfair Contract Terms Directive (UCTD).

---

[5] *Bogdan Matei, Ioana Ofelia Matei v. Volksbank Romania SA*, Case C-143/13.

Concerning this point, the CJEU said: "The Court has held that *contractual terms falling within the notion of the 'main subject-matter* of the contract', within the meaning of Article 4(2) of Directive 93/13, must be understood as being those *that lay down the essential obligations of the contract and, as such, characterise it.*" And concluded that "*[t]he mere fact that the 'risk charge' may be regarded as representing a relatively important part of the APR* and, therefore, the income received by the lender from the credit agreements concerned *is in principle irrelevant* for the purposes of determining whether the terms providing for that charge define the 'main subject-matter' of the contract".

Matei[6] seems to imply that the "core terms" notion is a formal, abstract one referring to the legal "characterization" of the type of contract the parties have entered into, and specifically based on whether such legal description categorizes the subject matter of the term as being essential or not.

Following this premise, the fact that a certain charge in a loan is included in the annual percentage rate (APR), even as a (quantitatively, one would imagine) noticeable portion of it, is irrelevant for determining whether the charge should be considered a core term or not. The APR is a tool intended to increase the salience of various components of cost in a transaction that is in itself complex, involves various dimensions and typically includes charges that are deferred or extended over time. In complex, multidimensional consumer contracts, one would expect firms trying to decrease the number of salient components and increase non-salient ones. Enhancing salience may result in better assessment of the true costs of a credit and more desirable consumer choices.[7]

There is evidence, however, that, despite the concentration of price information in the APR figure, and the fact that the APR simplifies in a standardized way some crucial information, results remain unimpressive in terms of improving consumer awareness and welfare.

Even when one is skeptical about the virtues of APR in increasing actual levels of salience for consumers in credit contracts, *Matei*'s utter disregard of the economic issues is troubling. The fact that a given charge is a major component of the APR should have a bearing—not necessarily decisive— on whether the charge was salient, and thus the consumer was reasonably

---

[6] Building upon a previous CJEU decision, *Arpad Kásler, Hajnalka Káslerné Rábai v. OTP Jegzálogbank Zrt*, Case C-26/13.

[7] See Bar-Gill (2008, p. 1140, 2014, p. 465).

aware of its existence and overall impact on the total cost of credit for her/ him. For sure, one could conclude that, given the available evidence, and the circumstances involved, the inclusion in the APR does not make that charge "sufficiently" salient or transparent for the consumer in terms of making an informed choice. But the general finding that whether a given price component is included or not in the APR is "irrelevant" for a finding of the "core term" exemption seems ill-advised from an economic perspective, especially when coupled with the assertion that what is a core term is something that has to be determined on the basis of what general contract law deems to be an "essential obligation" for a party. It is hard to question that the categories and words of civil codes are generally less correlated with salience than the inclusion or not by a certain price component in the APR.

In *Costea*,[8] a commercial lawyer signs a credit agreement with a bank. The repayment of that loan was secured by a mortgage over a building belonging to the lawyer's firm. The credit agreement was signed by him, not only as borrower but also as representative of his law firm, since the firm was the mortgagor securing repayment the loan.

The CJEU held, in order to solve the issue of whether the contract was a consumer contract, that the fact that the loan was secured by a mortgage granted by an experienced commercial lawyer in his capacity as representative of his law firm, and involving goods belonging to that firm, is irrelevant. Although in general there are plausible (legal and economic) grounds to disregard certain pieces of information in legal decision-making, *Costea* leaves one wondering about the reasons for discarding most of the case-specific information regarding the knowledge and position of the borrower and mortgagor, an attitude that may be thought to induce a cruder and less informed solution to consumer contract cases.

Another illustration is the *Gutierrez Naranjo*[9] case. With its decision in this case, the CJEU cast its powerful vote in the controversy surrounding the saga of the Spanish litigation on mortgage floor clauses (limits to the variability of adjustable mortgage rates) inserted in many mortgage loan agreements in Spain. When interest rates in the Eurozone started to decrease, reaching historically minimum rates, many Spanish debtors saw

---

[8] *Horatiu Ovidiu Costea v. Volksbank Romania SA*, Case C-110/14.

[9] *Francisco Gutiérrez Naranjo v. Cajasur Banco SAU, Ana María Palacios Martínez v. Banco Bilbao Vizcaya Argentaria SA (BBVA), Banco Popular Español v Emilio Irles López and Teresa Torres Andreu*, Joined Cases C-154/15, C-307/15 and C-308/15.

how their mortgage payments decreased but only limitedly so, resulting in monthly payments higher than the ones they would have faced had they been paying their monthly dues with respect to Euribor plus the agreed spread, with no lower bound or floor.

The Spanish Supreme Court held that these were subject to a material transparency control[10] as to whether the consumer could actually understand the full legal and economic consequences of the contract, and held them as unfair. However, in attention to a number of factors, the Spanish Court opted for limiting the restitutionary effects of the finding of unfairness. When the issue was referred by several Spanish lower courts, the CJEU ruled the Spanish Supreme Court position on limited restitution as incompatible with the UCTD. In *Gutiérrez Naranjo*, the CJEU found that "Article 6(1) of Directive 93/13 must be interpreted as meaning that a contractual term held to be unfair *must be regarded, in principle, as never having existed, so that it cannot have any effect on the consumer*". Thus, the effects of a finding of unfairness are automatic, almost robot-like. Once a term is held unfair, regardless of the underlying reasons, the subject matter covered by the term and the "severity" of the unfairness, there is no room for maneuver in the consequences for the parties. No economic (either theoretical or empirical, based on rational choice or behavioral) reason can be weighed as to the consequences of unfairness. Automatic legal consequences always ensue from finding a contract term unfair.

In *Gut Springheide*,[11] the CJEU crafted the EU normative notion of the "average consumer" and the defining features of such a notion. The "average consumer", created in order to assess the misleading potential of promotional materials for the sale of eggs, not only has been kept in the area of labeling and composition of food products (*Teekanne*[12]), but has now traveled to credit contracts (*Kásler, Matei*), and generalized to all commercial practices.

The CJEU is adamant in considering that the average consumer notion is not an empirical one, and that the conditions and features defining it in any given case result from courts exercising their own judgment to determine what the typical features of the average consumer will be. But if it is

---

[10] Already anticipated by the CJEU in *RWE Vertrieb AG v. Verbraucherzentrale Nordrhein-Westfalen e.V.*, Case C-92/11.

[11] *Gut Springheide GmbH and Rudolf Tusky v Oberkreisdirektor des Kreises Steinfurt*, Case C-210/96.

[12] *Bundesverband der Verbraucherzentralen und Verbraucherverbände – Verbraucherzentrale Bundesverband e.V. v Teekanne GmbH & Co. KG*, Case C-195/14.

not a statistical composite of how real individual consumers are and react, what is the average consumer? A normative aspiration? A moral claim? A backdoor to introduce a general due care standard for consumers? An *ad hoc* determination based on policy or, worse, expediency to move the unfairness threshold up or down as desired by the decision-maker? From an economic perspective, the benchmark should not be idealistic, but firmly grounded on how consumers really are and behave, not how they could or should act, based on some external normative criterion.

5.3   Contrasting Legal and Economic Mindsets for Economic Interactions

As already mentioned, the refinements in economic theory and economic empirics in recent decades have vastly transformed economics as an intellectual field. In contemporary societies, the complexity and reach of the law and legal institutions has also expanded to a considerable degree. These paths of expansion, however, have not fundamentally altered the intellectual gist either in economics or in law.

Despite the emergence of law and economics as a distinctive area of thinking over legal systems and their role in societies, and despite the more or less intense pushes of some law and economics efforts, legal thinking, at least in Europe and Latin America, has remained largely unaltered as to how the regulation of social interactions, including the market interactions over which the theoretical and empirical knowledge in economics has been accumulating and refining, should be conceived and undertaken.

The lack of influence from economic thinking is not an anecdote, or a specific oddity afflicting the CJEU and its members. The clear diffidence about economics in an area of the law squarely dealing with economic interactions is a reflection of certain features that characterize legal thinking in its traditional European manifestations. These internal factors, linked to the law's self-conception as an intellectual enterprise, are more relevant than other ideological or philosophical stances commonly raised in the face of economic knowledge.

One possible explanation (Schwartz 2011, pp. 1536–1537) for the situation (in the US) of lack of dialogue between pure contract law scholars on the one side and economists and economically trained legal scholars working in contract theory on the other is found in the joint effect of two forces: (i) modern contract theory is intrinsically complex and sophisticated, and the translation of the substance and implications of this body of knowledge for lay readers (such as legal scholars and judges) requires an amount of effort that has discouraged economists even from trying; and (ii) the prevailing and appalling "economic illiteracy" (Schwartz 2011, p. 1537) in the traditional contract law *professoriat*.

Others (Garoupa and Ulen 2008, p. 1555) would argue that the failure of economics to exert an influence over the law is highly dependent on the success (or lack thereof) of Law and Economics as a school of thought in legal academia. For this view, in addition to certain institutional conditions (a competitive market of institutions providing legal education, essentially law schools), a key point is the existence of a sufficiently established—albeit not necessarily dominant—"legal realism" movement among legal scholars. They understand "legal realism" as the combination of two major views: skepticism about legal formalist claims of internal consistency and self-sufficiency of legal rules and categories, and an interest in "law in action", that is, the actual effects of legal rules and their implementation on actual behavior and phenomena. They argue that both a competitive academic market and legal realism are necessary prerequisites for the success of law and economics as a new strand of legal thinking. And when law and economics becomes an accepted part of legal academia, economic input would naturally flow into the understanding and regulation of market interactions by legal rules and courts with the intermediation of legal academics.

In my account, however, I would like to emphasize the role of modes of thinking and conceptual apparatuses that I consider still dominant in traditional schools of European legal thinking. I concede that there is some variance in the authority that those intellectual forces have over legal systems, depending on factors that are specific to a given legal culture, and to observed practices in a given subset of legal academia.

The first of those features or properties could be labeled as the anti-realism, idealism or inward-looking bent in legal thinking. In contrast, economics could be characterized as dominated by a realist or outward-looking perspective, in the sense that economists typically conceive their task as giving an account of observed phenomena in real-world social interactions (see the contrast between Kelsen and Posner in Małecka 2017, pp. 498, 507).

The economic disciplinary outlook attempts to explain what is out there, searching for factors underlying why social interactions assume the form they do in reality. Legal thinking, quite differently, is commonly viewed as a discipline that tries to make sense (broadly conceived) of normative propositions that may be recognized and imposed as "Law" in a given time and place. The task of the legal enterprise is to reveal the scope and meaning of those propositions, expressed either as formal legal rules adopted by legislatures and other legitimate state authorities, or in the form of doctrines and interpretations of existing legal materials developed by courts and commentators (e.g., Larenz and Canaris 1995, p. 17). Even empirically oriented legal scholars, in the end, admit that legal research is a normative endeavor, and that its task is to give advice about normative propositions to those who have to adopt, enforce or interpret them (e.g., Engel 2018, p. 18). Many lawyers (doctrinal ones at least) would inhabit the "normative reality" and not the external reality of agents interacting in the real world. In a way, Hegel's dictum (*"Was sein soll, ist in der Tat auch"*) seems to be broadly shared in legal thinking, although perhaps not always consciously. Not all would endorse the belief (which would be an extreme version of legal idealism) in the internal integrity of the law and the ability to provide response to any question or issue that arises in the functioning of a legal system, but milder versions of this view would be common in many, if not most, legal cultures in Europe.

This does not imply that looking for explanations about the law is beyond the realm of legal thinking. It is not. In fact, explanatory theories abound in law and legal research, even in traditional and doctrinal legal scholarship. What is characteristic of explanatory ventures in legal thinking is that almost always the *explanandum* is not given by observations about external world events or actions (or stylized or intuitive generalizations about them), but instead by legal rules, decided cases or doctrinal interpretations (e.g., Wendel 2011, pp. 1062–1063). In economics, typically it is the external world, directly or through observations, generalizations or expectations concerning behavior, which constitutes the *explanandum* in the explanatory models or theories.

To be sure, in law and economics, sometimes the *explanandum* (or part of it at least) is also given by legal doctrines, materials or outcomes. In this sense, an economic model may be, *inter alia*, able (or conducive to) rationalize or explain legal doctrine, case law or even legislative solutions,[13] although not necessarily the internal reasons and arguments provided by courts (see Esposito 2020).

---

[13] Kornhauser (2018).

As to the *explanans*, explanatory inquiries in legal scholarship are commonly characterized by using hypotheses whose nature is also mostly "legal" or "internal" to the legal system. It could be argued that many elements that have become now "legal" or "internal" were borrowed in reality in the past from a varied set of disciplines: Theology, History, Philology, Philosophy (moral, political), Linguistics. And to this long and illustrious list of "external" disciplines providing inputs for explanations about legal doctrine, law and economics would simply try to add economics, in its various dimensions. It is true, however, that the inward-looking attraction remains strong, at least in certain areas or schools in legal academia.[14]

The contrasting intellectual outlooks of economics and traditional legal scholarship are almost naturally projected onto the research questions posed by one and the other in the common areas of interest. If one thinks of contracts, the dominant legal scholarship typically starts by asking questions about the meaning of the normative propositions that have validity in a given legal system to govern contracts, and the ways in which case law developed by courts and commentary by legal scholars help to ascribe one or the other meaning to the texts, or to complement the shortcomings of the latter with respect to certain situations or cases, real or imagined. The economic approach would start and proceed very differently. It would look into what contracts the parties write and what contracting practices are observed between the parties, what problems the parties are trying to address with those terms and practices and how the solutions implemented may compare with some other feasible arrangements that could be implementable. Eventually the legal system would be added to the picture, and the main questions to ask would be of the following kind: what can the law do to help the parties achieve their ends through contracting? How does the law actually perform this function?[15]

A second feature of how most participants in European legal culture perceive their task and role is linked to the notion of essentialism (or anti-instrumentalism) of law (or large portions of it, at least). As a consequence, essentialism will extend to legal rules and also to legal concepts, both those explicit in the law and those "constructed" by legal scholarship.

---

[14] See, for instance, the treatment of "goals or functions" and of the "*Natur der Sache*" in legal methodology, in Larenz and Canaris (1995, pp. 153 and 236).

[15] See Kornhauser and MacLeod (2013, p. 918).

Law is often conceived by lawyers in most legal professions and activities (including academia) as an inescapable, and not contingent, building block of an intrinsically (and perhaps objectively) valuable framework for the realization of certain ultimate social values.

This belief about the entire edifice of the law and its associated value and virtue is then transposed to widely accepted legal concepts and categories that cease to be seen as means to achieve an end (even an internal one to the legal edifice itself). Thus, they are not viewed as "mere tools" to achieve goals (to better understand the world, or to act upon it), but as possessing intrinsic value, linked to ultimate or inherent values of the legal system. Paraphrasing William James,[16] for part of traditional European legal culture one could say that legal theories and concepts are often viewed as answers to permanent enigmas in the law, on whose truth we can safely rest.

In economics, theories are simply instruments to provide (hopefully satisfactory) explanations about external realities. Quite differently from traditional self-conceptions in law, economics is typically conceived by the economics profession as a scholarly endeavor devoid of any intrinsic value beyond its capacity to provide useful explanations about the observed phenomena of interest to its practitioners. Its core value lies in the ability to predict outcomes and explain observed phenomena. To be sure, there is (and always has been, since economics has a distinct intellectual character) a policy side to the enterprise of economics as a discipline, but it is conceived as "added" or external to its main explanatory mission. Moreover, this policy dimension lies in providing the theoretical and empirical tools to explain and predict behavior and outcomes in the real world that could serve policymakers to take more informed decisions in the pursuit of its goals or ultimate objectives.

One would then see without surprise the reluctance by legal thinkers and scholars and, inspired by them, courts and practitioners, to replace (or even, more modestly, to contrast or to supplement) the legal notions, doctrines and categories containing and expressing intrinsic worth, with theoretical models and predictions, and with empirical evidence about outcomes that admittedly lack the intrinsic values that the legal categories allegedly possess.

With respect to the third feature I would like to emphasize, it is fair to start with the assertion that in certain areas of European legal scholarship

---

[16]James (1992, p. 42).

it is still a prevalent perspective—perhaps even dominant in some influential national legal cultures—that legal thinking approaches its object of interest (the law and legal institutions) through internal comprehension or interpretive individual understanding (*Verstehen*) and not through external explanation trying to discern and establish general causal claims or propositions about the validity of a hypothesis for the outcome in need of explanation (*Erklären*; Larenz and Canaris 1995, p. 25). Legal scholarship (or legal science, as certain legal cultures call it) belongs to the world of internal understanding; economics (and law and economics) belongs to that of external explanation.

In this view, as a result, methods of quantification, of searching for causal connections between externally observed phenomena and factors or variables, are seen as alien to the true enterprise of legal scholarship. Moreover, the idea that problems or debates may not have a theoretical answer (i.e., theory does not offer a determinate view of what is the best explanation among the competing ones) and only an empirical one[17] seems to be alien to predominant legal thinking, according to which empirics providing the clue to what the law should be is at odds with the deeply entrenched idea that law possesses internal values and an internal logic that is not contingent upon facts.

True, if legal scholarship has to provide advice to legal decision-makers, prediction of the outcomes over some variable of interest becomes a relevant issue, and causal inference enters legal thinking (Engel 2018, p. 7). However, for this one needs to assume that the law should care for the outcomes in the real world, which is not obvious to everyone in law and legal thinking (on consequence-based legal reasoning, see Cserne 2020).

In economics, in contrast, and especially in recent years, there is an emphasis on using data (from real-world interactions, natural experiments, field experiments or laboratory experiments) to answer questions about the causal effects of certain factors or variables. Correspondingly, data analysis and statistical inference loom very large in the economic profession. As a consequence, empirical methods often hold the key to resolving

---

[17] I am aware of the Is/Ought dilemma, and I do not claim that a reliable bridge between empirical findings and normative conclusions always (or even often) exists. But not rarely, both in law and in law and economics, the research question does not lie with ultimate goals or normative justifications for an action or policy, but merely on how to best achieve a shared or undisputed normative goal.

debates about conflicting predictions and implications from otherwise well-conceived and executed theoretical models.

In sum, deeply held conceptions in Europe as to the nature and role of legal thinking and the entire enterprise of the legal system may—and in my view they do—lead one to look into economic concepts, arguments and evidence to help the functioning of the laws and legal institutions dealing with economic interactions and markets. The cases examined in Sect. 5.2 should not be perceived as isolated instances of short-sighted decisions on how to regulate market interactions, but the reflection of an important, deeper, perhaps structural, lack of receptiveness of standard European legal thinking toward realist, instrumentalist and empiricist views of complex systems (such as the law).

5.4   Conclusions

The lack of resonance of the contributions—both theoretical and empirical—from economics in the European legal community, case law and practice is, I believe, a very unfortunate situation. Economists often lack the deep knowledge of legal issues to formulate good questions about the functioning of law and the social and economic relevance of legal rules and institutions. In turn, lawyers, who do possess such knowledge, often lack proper tools to answer deep questions about the functioning of law and how it affects firms, consumers and society at large.

In my years as a legal scholar, I have come to observe, and now hold as a firm belief, that legal scholarship and the entire endeavor behind legal systems would significantly improve with the intelligent and discerning use of the contributions from economics. But deeply—almost sacredly among some—held convictions in the European legal community seem to raise significant obstacles for such a development. And until these beliefs significantly lose appeal, it is hard to anticipate that economic input, despite its intellectual allure, will become a major factor in shaping legal thinking and legal policy over market interactions, at least among courts and legal scholarship in connection with major legal areas such as contract and consumer law, tort law, administrative law and several others.

Obviously, the more "refined" and more "institution-attentive" economic contributions become, the easier is their way into legal thinking, and the higher the chances that the legal community will be responsive to their findings. I do not deny that much can be improved in this respect in order to make economic input not only more "user-friendly" for non-economists, but also more targeted to the relevant questions in law. However, I fear that these intellectual obstacles in the dominant legal mindset are likely to prove resilient even *vis-à-vis* more sophisticated and more legally alert and conscious economic contributions to understand the role and effects of legal systems in governing social and economic interactions.

For instance, the clear advances over the relatively unsophisticated views of price theory in the 1960s and early 1970s[18] have not made significant progress in European legal academia. Even the warm welcome to behavioral economics in influential tenets of the European legal academia may be explained, perhaps, by a—however misguided—view[19] that behavioral economics is largely a refutation of standard microeconomics and game theory: in reality, it is for the most part a refinement of the existing approach by scholars who consider themselves professional economists.[20]

For this (sad) state of affairs in European legal systems to change for the better, the initial push needs to come from legal scholarship.

References

Alemanno, Alberto, and Anne-Lise Sibony. 2015. The Emergence of Behavioural Policy-Making: A European Perspective. In *Nudge and the Law: A European Perspective*, ed. Alberto Alemanno and Anne-Lise Sibony, 1–25. Oxford: Hart Publishing.

Bar-Gill, Oren. 2008. The Law, Economics and Psychology of Subprime Mortgage Contracts. *Cornell Law Review* 94: 8–59.

———. 2014. Consumer Transactions. In *The Oxford Handbook of Behavioral Economics and the Law*, ed. Eyal Zamir and Doron Teichman, 465–489. Oxford: Oxford University Press.

---

[18] A period in which the three major agents in economic interactions (consumers, firms and the government) were treated almost as black boxes beyond analysis: consumer tastes are given, firms exist to maximize profits, and governments are benevolent agents of citizens and the common good: Sandler (2001, p. 95).

[19] Alemanno and Sibony (2015, pp. 22–23). Critically on this view, Esposito (2015, p. 257). For different reasons, others are critical with the use of behavioral economics to explain legally relevant behavior and legal institutions (Leeson 2019, p. 30) or advise caution to legal scholars in order not to misuse behavioral economics (Zeiler 2019, p. 22).

[20] This is the prevalent view among many of the most representative behavioral economists themselves: Laibson and List (2015, p. 385).

Calabresi, Guido. 2016. *The Future of Law & Economics*. New Haven: Yale University Press.

Coase, Ronald. 1988. *The Firm, the Market and the Law*. Chicago: University of Chicago Press.

———. 1994. *Essays on Economics and Economists*. Chicago: University of Chicago Press.

Cserne, Péter. 2020. Economic Approaches to Legal Reasoning: An Overview. In *Economics in Legal Reasoning*, ed. Péter Cserne and Fabrizio Esposito, 25–41. London: Palgrave Macmillan.

Engel, Christoph. 2018. Empirical Methods for the Law. *Journal of Institutional and Theoretical Economics* 174: 5–23.

Esposito, Fabrizio. 2015. Book Review: Nudge and the Law. *Humana.Mente Journal of Philosophical Studies* 28: 255–274.

———. 2020. Reverse Engineering Legal Reasoning. In *Economics in Legal Reasoning*, ed. Péter Cserne and Fabrizio Esposito, 139–154. London: Palgrave Macmillan.

Franck, Jens-Uwe. 2017. Law-Making and Adjudication for the Internal Market: The Role of Economic Reasoning. In *European Legal Methodology*, ed. Karl Riesenhuber. Cambridge: Intersentia.

Garoupa, Nuno. 2012. Ronald Coase and Law and Economics in Europe. *International Review of Economics* 59: 223–229.

Garoupa, Nuno, and Thomas Ulen. 2008. The Market for Legal Innovation: Law and Economics in Europe and the United States. *Alabama Law Review* 59: 1555–1563.

James, William. 1992. Pragmatism. In *William James. Pragmatism in Focus*, ed. Doris Olin. Abingdon: Routledge.

Kornhauser, Lewis. 2018. A Tale of Two Models: Formal Theory in Economic Analysis of Law. *Working Paper*. New York University School of Law.

Kornhauser, Lewis, and W. Bentley MacLeod. 2013. Contracts between Legal Persons. In *Handbook of Organizational Economics*, ed. Robert Gibbons and John Roberts, 918–957. Princeton: Princeton University Press.

Laibson, David, and John A. List. 2015. Principles of Behavioral Economics. *American Economic Review Papers & Proceedings* 105: 385–390.

Larenz, Karl, and Claus-Wilhelm Canaris. 1995. *Methodenlehre der Rechtswissenschaft*. 3rd ed. Dordrecht: Springer.

Leeson, Peter T. 2019. Do We Need Behavioral Economics to Explain Law? *European Journal of Law and Economics* 48: 29–42.

Małecka, Magdalena. 2017. Posner versus Kelsen: The Challenges for Scientific Analysis of Law. *European Journal of Law and Economics* 43: 495–516.

Mathis, Klaus, and Avishalom Tor, eds. 2016. *Nudging: Possibilities, Limitations and Applications in European Law and Economics*. Dordrecht: Springer.

Micklitz, Hans-W, Anne-Lise Sibony, and Fabrizio Esposito, eds. 2018. *Research Methods in Consumer Law. A Handbook.* Cheltenham: Edward Elgar.

Sandler, Todd. 2001. *Economic Concepts for the Social Sciences.* Cambridge, MA: Cambridge University Press.

Schwartz, Alan. 2011. Two Culture Problems in Law and Economics. *University of Illinois Law Review* 5: 1531–1550.

Wendel, W. Bradley. 2011. Explanation in Legal Scholarship: The Inferential Structure of Doctrinal Legal Analysis. *Cornell Law Review* 96: 1035–1074.

Zeiler, Kathryn. 2019. Mistaken about Mistakes. *European Journal of Law and Economics* 48: 9–27.

PART III

Economics and Fact-Finding

CHAPTER 6

What Is Forensic Economics?

Jan Broulík

Abstract This chapter provides an overview of forensic economics by discussing four questions about its domain. The first question asks whether forensic economics is a practical or academic enterprise, or both. The second one concerns the types of legal decisions that forensic economics informs, including three separate stages of law enforcement and the distinction between questions of fact and law. The third question relates to the fields of law to which forensic economics applies with special attention to tort damages and antitrust. And the fourth one considers the position of the people who carry out the forensic-economic analyses outside of or within an enforcement body.

Keywords Forensic economics • Enforcement • Fact-finding • Tort law • Antitrust law

---

I would like to thank the editors for their helpful comments.

J. Broulík (✉)
Faculty of Law, University of Amsterdam, Amsterdam, The Netherlands
e-mail: j.broulik@uva.nl

© The Author(s) 2020
P. Cserne, F. Esposito (eds.), *Economics in Legal Reasoning*,
Palgrave Studies in Institutions, Economics and Law,
https://doi.org/10.1007/978-3-030-40168-9_6

6.1   Introduction

While it is universally agreed that economics has a forensic branch, no such consensus exists as to what it exactly entails (Christiansen and Ewald 2014, p. 144). This chapter provides an overview of *forensic economics*, discussing the four following questions: Is it a practical or/and an academic enterprise? What types of legal decisions does it inform? Which fields of law accommodate it? Who performs it? Examination of these questions provides insight not only into the concept and practice of forensic economics but also into the interaction between economics and law more generally. The chapter draws significantly on scholarship concerning the economic determination of tort damages as well as the literature on antitrust economics, complemented by a wide range of other writings.

6.2   Practical and/or Academic Enterprise?

6.2.1   Forensic Economics Is Primarily Practical

Forensic economics—as all scientific disciplines—generates knowledge on the subject under study. An important issue to consider with respect to forensic economics is the purpose for which knowledge happens to be generated. Generally speaking, one may seek knowledge for its own sake (academic reason) or to answer the question "what is to be done?" (practical reason). In the context of law, the practical reason takes a particular form—knowledge is sought in order to inform the creation or the enforcement of legal rules (legal decision-making). This duality of reason has been recognized, for instance, by Jaffe (1955, p. 244) with respect to fact-finding in general: "The finding is made for a purpose or function. It may be simply for understanding or putting our world in order. It may be, as is true of the law, in order to lay the basis for the exercise of power."

These two purposes may also lie behind any instance of economic analysis: it may be conducted in order to improve our understanding of a certain aspect of reality or to inform a particular legal decision (see Lanneau 2014, p. 26). Forensic economics is primarily about the latter (or a subset thereof). Many commentators in this vein draw a contrast between forensic economics on the one hand and economic research in academic context on the other (e.g. Christiansen and Ewald 2014, p. 145; Gavil 2008, p. 199; Lianos 2010, p. 230; Lianos and Genakos 2013, p. 116). Also, virtually all perspectives on forensic economics that will be discussed assume a practical character of the discipline. An economic analysis is thus not considered forensic unless it is carried out in order to inform legal decision-making.[1]

To be sure, the line between academic and practical analysis may be sometimes rather fuzzy because, even if an analysis is not actually carried out for a legal decision-maker, it could still address a more or less practical problem and, consequently, a law-maker or law-enforcer might rely on its findings. Yet, there usually are differences between the two types of analyses, the most distinctive factor being the numerous constraints faced by economic analyses informing legal decision-making. To give an example, although the law may to some extent facilitate access to data (Gerber 2009, pp. 35–37), economic inquiries informing legal decision-making tend to work with poorer input than academic analyses (Ireland 1997, p. 64); for instance, as observed by Hovenkamp (2005, p. 46), "[e]conomists [in academia] often select markets for study because data gathering in them is particularly easy or other characteristics of the market tend to simplify economic analysis. By contrast, the markets for antitrust litigation are selected by plaintiffs, who pay scant attention to their complexity or may even regard it as advantageous." Forensic analyses are also typically greatly limited by time (Christiansen and Ewald 2014, p. 146). The most essential constraint is then the law itself—this issue will be discussed in the context of law enforcement.

6.2.2   Academic Forensic Economics

The fact that forensic economics is primarily a practical enterprise does not mean that it has no academic branch. Consider, for instance, the *Journal of Forensic Economics* published by the US-based National Association of Forensic Economics (NAFE), which features scholarship that "grew out of a desire by professional economic consultants and expert witnesses to establish contact with each other to discuss common problems" (Ireland 1997, p. 67). This scholarship is usually written by experts combining academic with practical work and serves as a foundation for many forensic economic opinions (Ward 2014, p. 9). Another example is "applied economic research targeted to the specific matters that arise in competition law proceedings" (Decker 2009, p. 179) published in other venues. In

---

[1] An analysis may inform legal decision-making through guiding other analyses, which, in turn, inform legal decisions; see the following section.

other words, forensic-economic scholarship—rather than advancing knowledge for its own sake—aims to guide the practical analyses (see Tinari 2016b, p. 1).[2]

To summarize, there is virtually unanimous agreement that forensic economics is first and foremost a practical enterprise providing information required in order to make legal decisions.[3] Its eventual academic branch is merely secondary and subordinate to this primary objective. That is why the remainder of this chapter will focus mainly on the decision-making use of economics.

6.3   TYPE OF DECISION

6.3.1   Law-Making versus Enforcement

Before discussing the role of economics in legal decision-making, it is necessary to specify what is meant by a legal decision in the present context. There are two general categories of decisions concerning law: those that make—or repeal or amend—legal rules (law-making) and those that apply the rules in order to enforce them (law enforcement). The former category includes, for instance, adoption of statutes by the legislature or delegated law-making by administrative agencies. Law enforcement, also known as law application or adjudication, by contrast entails administration of legal rules to individual cases by courts, agencies and other competent bodies.

Economics used in law enforcement is generally considered forensic. It is, however, an open question whether also economics used in law-making ought to qualify as such. On the one hand, there are voices in favor, including several commentators from the antitrust camp (Christiansen and

---

[2] See Danziger and Katz (2019) as an example of such scholarship.

[3] A notable exception to the idea that forensic economics relates to legal decision-making is presented by Zitzewitz (2012). Zitzewitz operates with the term "academic forensic economics" when referring to economic analyses "carried out in order to advance the general understanding" of a particular category of social phenomena, that is, not in order to—even vicariously—inform legal decision-making. He in particular focuses on economic detection and quantification of behavior which agents would prefer to conceal because of its unlawfulness and which is at the same time important to the functioning of the economy. He does not explain why economic analyses carried out in order to advance the general understanding of other law-related phenomena, such as economic consequences of traffic accidents, should not count as academic forensic economics. It is also far from clear what is to be gained by clustering this type of academic research under the rubric of forensic economics.

Ewald 2014, p. 154; Connor 2008, p. 31; Schinkel 2008, p. 6). These authors thus use the forensic label for any practical application of economics to law. On the other hand, if we look at forensic science in general, it is usually understood as science that informs resolution of individual legal cases. Science used in law-making is then usually referred to by other terms such as science of public policy or regulatory science. This distinguishing between the two types of practical economic analyses appears to be motivated by the fact that the enforcement and law-making settings differ in various relevant aspects. In this chapter I follow the latter view and focus only on economics serving law enforcement.

6.3.2   Enforcement and Its Stages

As mentioned, the competence to enforce legal rules may be enjoyed by a variety of bodies. Although some commentators confine forensic economics only to resolution of cases within courtroom litigation (e.g. Tinari 2010, p. 398), there is no compelling reason why one should not count as forensic also the use of economics in enforcement proceedings run by non-court bodies, including not only adversarial but also inquisitorial proceedings. To give an example, when a European national antitrust agency, such as the German *Bundeskartellamt*, relies on economic analysis while applying law to an individual case in which it acts as both prosecutor and decision-maker, this analysis may also be seen as forensic (see, for example, Christiansen and Ewald 2014; Schinkel 2008).

Law enforcement consists of up to three distinct stages (see Kovacic and Hyman 2012, p. 535). First, whereas some enforcers are supplied with cases externally—for example by plaintiffs and complainants—others may need to detect suspect conduct on their own. Second, the core of law enforcement is the actual assessment of whether the conduct in question is lawful or unlawful; Hart (1994, pp. 96–97) calls this liability-centered stage the "minimal form of adjudication". Third, finding of an infringement usually triggers an additional stage consisting in the specification of a remedy, such as damages or a fine. The following paragraphs consider the applicability of economics within each of these stages.

The detection stage of enforcement may in some cases rely on economics. As a matter of fact, the definition of forensic economics adopted by the NAFE includes economics-based fraud detection as an example (see also Zitzewitz 2012, p. 731). To give an illustration from the decision-making practice, Schinkel (2008, pp. 7–10) explains that economic tools are used to find a potential antitrust violation by systematically screening the market; a violation is indicated, for instance, by a decrease in price volatility over time, correlated capacity investments or sudden atypical changes in sales conditions or product quality (see also Röller 2005, p. 19). Given the specificity of this enforcement stage and the relative rarity of using economics in it, the remainder of this part focuses only on the two subsequent stages.

Also the stage at which the enforcer assesses whether law has been breached may be informed by economic findings (e.g. Ireland 2016, p. 261). For instance, the assessment of lawfulness of a business practice represents the main habitat of antitrust economic analyses. Another example is provided by Tinari (2010, p. 406): "In certain discrimination cases, economists or statisticians may be retained to analyze the hiring/firing patterns of an employer. This type of analysis is used to assist the client in the liability phase of a case." Nevertheless, note that liability gets often decided without any economic input, even if the following remedial stage is economics-based (see Tinari 2010, p. 399).

The last enforcement stage concerns the specification of remedies. Some commentators focusing on civil litigation associate forensic economics only with this stage, and in particular with the quantification of damages. For instance, Ireland (1997, p. 64) argues that forensic economics equals "the economics of measurement and projection of damages". Nevertheless, economics may also prove useful in the specification of remedies other than damages, such as in "formulation and imposition of penalties and remedies" in antitrust law (Brunt 1999, p. 358).

6.3.3   Questions of Law and Fact

A crucial aspect of using economics—and other sciences—within law enforcement concerns the distinction between questions of fact and questions of law (cf. Canale and Tuzet 2020; Hubková 2020).[4] In a nutshell, the role of an enforcer is to base her/his decision on what happened, or sometimes will happen (see, for example, Landes and Posner 1994), in the particular case at hand (question of fact) as well as on the law governing the case (question of law). The enforcer determines both the applicable law and the facts of the case, and then applies the former to the latter in

---

[4] Note that the terminology is not settled in this context.

order to arrive at a decision.[5] These steps take place as part of the assessment of lawfulness as well as at the remedial stage. To establish whether there is an infringement, the enforcer determines the content of the substantive legal rule that governs the case and then the facts of the case that are relevant under this rule. If there is an infringement, the enforcer further determines the applicable remedial rule and the relevant facts in order to grant the prescribed remedy.

Hence, if economics is used to resolve questions of fact, it—"[t]aking the law as given" (Ward and Olson 1987, p. 2)—helps with the determination of facts relevant under the law (see Tinari 2010, p. 405). Whether economics will actually be used to determine a particular fact depends on whether it is suitable to the purpose and whether procedural rules allow its use (see later). Let us consider examples of economics-based resolution of a question of fact within the liability and remedial enforcement stages. If we think about the former stage, antitrust rules frequently stipulate that the lawfulness of a market practice depends on the share that the respective business holds in the relevant market. When such a rule gets applied to a particular case, it is necessary to determine, as one of the facts of the case, what the relevant market is. An economics-based determination of the relevant market thus represents a resolution of a question of fact (see Stigler 1992, p. 467). As regards the remedial stage, we may illustrate the economics-based resolution of questions of fact on the example of damages. Legal rules governing damages usually provide that the amount to be awarded correspond with the harm suffered. A fact relevant under such a rule is thus the extent of the harm,[6] and economics may in some jurisdictions be used to resolve it (see Klevorick 1975, p. 237).

Economics may also inform the resolution of a question of law (see, for example, Schinkel 2008, p. 6; Sibony 2012, p. 40), which may take the form of interpretation or adjudicative making of the law. This use of economics will be less common because the content of the rule will in most enforcement cases be clear and acceptable (see, for example, Schauer 1985),[7] requiring thus no interpretation or modification; and even if the

---

[5] As explained by Hart and Sacks (1994, p. 351), the two steps in reality take place simultaneously: "[T]he law determines what facts are relevant while at the same time the facts determine what law is relevant."

[6] That is why those who associate forensic economics with determination of damages may define it as "the application of economics to the ... quantification of harm from behavior that has become the subject of litigation" (Zitzewitz 2012, p. 731).

[7] This applies also to vague statutory formulations that have been clarified by case law.

enforcer actually does need to interpret the rule, other—noneconomic—
methods of interpretation might be more appropriate (see Canale and
Tuzet 2020). To nevertheless give an example, in the US antitrust case
Leegin, economic findings concerning the competitive effects of resale
price maintenance were used to overturn a precedent governing this market practice.[8]

There is a substantial difference between economic analyses concerning
a fact relevant under an applicable legal rule and the content of a legal rule.
They address distinct issues and, thus, take into account distinct considerations. The difference between the two categories of analysis is recognized, for instance, by Dunoff and Trachtman (1999, pp. 6–7), who call
the former economic analysis *in* law and the latter economic analysis *of* law
(see also Breyer 1983, p. 295; Klevorick 1975, pp. 237–239; Stigler 1992,
pp. 466–467).[9] It is noteworthy that this categorization suggests that
inquiries informing resolution of enforcement questions of law are materi-
ally distant from those that concern resolution of questions of fact but
close to those that have to do with (legislative or administrative) law-
making. This reflects the fact that the economic considerations to be taken
into account, for example, when a legislature adopts an antitrust rule and
when a court interprets it are largely identical; very similar economic factors are logically relevant. One may, therefore, wonder whether not only
analyses concerning questions of fact should be considered truly forensic.

6.3.4   Economics and Questions of Fact

Economic analyses informing enforcement questions of fact display
marked characteristics. First of all, each enforcement case is unique in the
sense that the facts constituting it are unique. Every case of pedestrian
injury caused by negligent driving is defined by a different pedestrian,
driver, location and time. Every abuse of dominance concerns a different
dominant business, abusive practice, product market, geographical market
and time. What this means is that law enforcement is based on the determination of specific rather than general facts. Forensic economics needs to
deliver such facts (see Tinari 2010, p. 389) whereas academic science—
including economics—usually seeks to capture generalities that recur in

---

[8] *Leegin Creative Leather Products, Inc. v. PSKS, Inc.*, 551 U.S. 877 (2007).
[9] It should be noted that the commentary mostly does not differentiate between academic
and practical economic inquiries into the content of the law (i.e. economic analysis of law).

the world (see, for example, Jasanoff 2005, p. S52).[10] The individual character of facts that forensic economics aspires to determine represents its most distinctive feature.

Further, the determination of facts is significantly shaped by the law as such (Ireland 1997, p. 64; Schap 2010b, p. 346; Tinari 2010, p. 399). This shaping takes two forms. First, the task of forensic economics is to determine those facts that are relevant under the applicable legal rules. This may on the one hand mean that the economic analysis is circumscribed by these rules—if the law does not consider a certain factor relevant, the person executing the analysis cannot take it into account even though he or she otherwise would (Aubuchon 2009, p. 71). For instance, some legal systems "do not allow economists to add past interest to losses that have occurred in the past" even though economic logic would suggest doing so (Ireland 2016, p. 261). Conversely, the law may also necessitate information on issues that academic economists consider irrelevant. By way of example, consider the so-called relevant market, the determination of which marks an essential step in most antitrust cases. While this determination is usually performed by economists, "[t]he question of what is 'the' relevant market never arises in economics outside of antitrust" enforcement (Fisher 2008, p. 132).

Second, the law also directly regulates the process through which a question of fact is to be resolved. To illustrate, a legal rule may prescribe the method through which the defendant's harm or the relevant market is to be determined in a case. There will also often be more general procedural rules, specifying, for instance, which evidence is admissible (see, for example, Giocoli 2020). In short, in law enforcement, "the methods of economics become tools to be applied according to the rules and procedures of the institutions and organizations that use them" (Gerber 2009, p. 24).[11]

---

[10] In forensic antitrust economics, this gets often discussed as the problem of identification of the right economic model (see Giocoli 2020, p. 114).

[11] Note that resolution of questions of fact tends to be much more heavily regulated than resolution of questions of law (see, for example, Cappalli 2002, p. 100).

6.4   FIELD OF LAW

6.4.1   Torts and Other Traditional Fields

Another dimension of forensic economics to consider is the field of law to which economics gets applied. At least in the United States, the great majority of published scholarship as well as practical analyses that bear the forensic-economic label concern tort law.[12] The two types of tort cases to which forensic economics pays most attention are personal injury and wrongful death (Schap 2010a, p. 347). These cases occupy the bulk of articles featured in the *Journal of Forensic Economics* (Ireland 1997, p. 65; Ward 2014, p. 8).

Nevertheless, forensic economics traditionally includes the application of economics also to other civil cases. Tinari (2010, p. 398) gives employment termination and breach of contract as examples of such cases. Ireland (1997, p. 65) further mentions "divorce, business valuation, employment discrimination and some analysis of commercial litigation". A similar list is provided by Ward (2014, p. 6): "commercial litigation, employment litigation, marital and property disputes". Additionally, Schap (2010a, p. 347) refers, for instance, to business valuation and lost profits, marital dissolution and workplace discrimination.

Publications that are explicitly called or generally understood as forensic-economic feature discussions of economic analyses applicable to all these types of cases. Such academic periodicals include, in addition to the *Journal of Forensic Economics*, mainly the *Journal of Legal Economics* run by the American Academy of Economic and Financial Experts, and the *Litigation Economic Review*, originally known as the *Legal Economic Digest*, published between 1995 and 2003 by NAFE (Tinari 2016b, p. 6; Ward 2014, p. 6). There are also many books addressing the application of economics to civil litigation such as Tinari (2016a) and Stephenson and Macpherson (2019).

6.4.2   Antitrust as a Nontraditional Field

By contrast, economics used in other legal fields, such as antitrust, is not labeled as forensic under the mainstream view. Granted, the definition of

---

[12] This is reflected, for instance, by the JEL Code assigned to the said scholarship: "K13—Tort Law and Product Liability; Forensic Economics".

forensic economics presented on NAFE's website does mention antitrust cases and also the research agenda set more than three decades ago in the very first issue of the *Journal of Forensic Economics* did include antitrust economics (see Ward and Olson 1987, p. 3). However, none of the forensic-economic journals has in reality featured more than a handful of pieces discussing the application of economics in antirust cases, and the most prominent experts working on antitrust cases are not NAFE members (Thornton and Ward 1999, p. 103). Ireland (1997, p. 65) comments on this exclusion of antitrust economics as follows: "In terms of published research and papers presented, antitrust law and the role economists play in antitrust litigation, while technically included within any reasonable definition of forensic economics, is really a subfield unto itself ... rather than ... forensic economics". A similar argument is advanced by Schap (2010a, p. 347): "Conceived of as economics applied to legal matters, forensic economics is a broad field indeed. Some applications that could fall under such a rubric, for example antitrust ..., for tradition's sake continue to be classified under other fields within economics."

These quotes reveal that economics informing antitrust enforcement is, analytically speaking, forensic. What is more, a great number of antitrust scholars do refer to it as such (e.g. Christiansen and Ewald 2014; Connor 2008; Decker 2009; Eden et al. 1985; Gavil 2008; Hovenkamp 2017; Schinkel 2008). One may hence wonder what motivates other commentators to exclude it. The main reason appears to be that antitrust issues "require a significantly different and specialized set of skills and knowledge, quite different from the methods used in personal and commercial cases" (Tinari 2016b, p. 3). This could be to some extent surprising because the economic analyses carried out in personal and commercial cases in fact build on a wide range of economic subfields (Brookshire 1991, p. 294) including price theory, labor economics and financial economics (Ireland 1997, p. 62; Thornton and Ward 1999, pp. 101–102); nevertheless, according to the presented logic, these analyses are methodologically still closer to each other than to antitrust analyses. The subfield of economics applicable to antitrust issues is the so-called industrial organization (Blair and Sokol 2015, p. xiii; Christiansen and Ewald 2014, p. 143), which is also why some authors—instead of forensic antitrust economics (e.g. Connor 2008, p. 42; Lianos 2010, p. 256) or forensic economics in competition law (e.g. Christiansen and Ewald 2014, p. 144; Lianos 2012)—speak about forensic industrial organization (e.g. Decker 2009, p. 197; Schinkel 2008, pp. 3–4). In short, economics informing antitrust enforcement appears to be often excluded from forensic economics because it requires different expertise than the more traditional cases.

While there are clear benefits to specialization, I do not see why the forensic label is to be usurped by only a subset of enforcement applications of economics. To be sure, economics used in civil cases may be content-wise so distant from other applications of economics to legal decision-making that there is not much point in running joint publication venues or professional associations. The term forensic economics should, however, in my view refer to economics applied to any legal field. From an analytical perspective, the "forensicity" of economics—or, for that matter, of any scientific discipline—has nothing to do with the divides between different fields of law (and the eventual associated divides between different subfields of economics); it refers to the use of economics within law enforcement. Moreover, as mentioned earlier, there are also practical concerns shared by any application of economics to facts of enforcement cases—be it the determination of damages or of the competitive effects of a merger—that will occasionally require lumping all these applications together. These concerns pertain to how methods of economics can be transferred from the academic setting to the context of law application characterized by fact specificity, and to the procedural rules governing the enforcement use of economics.

6.5   PERSONAL DIMENSION

The last dimension of forensic economics that this chapter will discuss concerns the people who carry out the economic analyses of case facts.[13] Forensic economics is often identified with experts delivering a testimony to a court (see, for example, Tinari 2010). It should, however, not be forgotten that expert opinions may serve as evidence also in non-court enforcement proceedings, such as those in antitrust cases in front of the European Commission. A broader understanding of forensic economics is thus possible as economics informing any enforcement case through an expert testimony. The prominent role of expert witnesses in forensic

---

[13] It might be worth adding that a rather idiosyncratic definition of forensic economics has been advanced by Ireland (1997, p. 64), according to whom the discipline amounts to "economics of economists as economic experts in litigation". While analyses of the incentives faced by practicing forensic economists and of their consequences may generate curious insights (see, for example, Froeb et al. 2009), they are not forensic unless they inform law enforcement.

economics is evidenced, for instance, by the fact that NAFE is "an organization created by expert witnesses" (Rodgers and Weinstein 2014, p. 175) who had been "involved in expert testimony involving economics" (Brookshire 2003, p. 23).

Understanding forensic economics as a provision of economic testimony to an enforcement body by experts external to the body amounts to viewing it as a private industry (cf. Brookshire et al. 1990; Connor 2008). This is because expert witness testimonies are provided through a market,[14] where they may be commissioned either by a party to an enforcement proceeding or by the enforcer itself (Zitzewitz 2012, p. 731). This business understanding of forensic economics is adopted, for instance, by Tinari (2010, p. 404), according to whom "[e]ntering the world of forensic economics implies that the economist will be involved in a 'practice', that is, a small business". A similar portrayal is provided by Schap (2010b, pp. 345–346): "[Forensic economists] have practices that range from the full-time academic economist involved in a relatively small number of assignments per year to the full-time independent [forensic economist] practicing solo who participates in dozens of cases annually to the large forensic economics firm where several [forensic economists] collectively handle hundreds of case assignments each year." This categorization holds also for forensic antitrust economics (Connor 2008, p. 41), where the largest firms employ hundreds of economists.

Economics-based determination of case facts is nevertheless not always carried out only by external experts hired mostly by litigants but sometimes also by people working inside the enforcement institutions. As regards antitrust, for instance, economists strongly populate enforcement agencies (e.g. Padilla 2015) and may even act as—perhaps rather specialized—judges or their clerks (e.g. Lianos 2010, pp. 262–263). Since the enforcement carried out by these economists concerns individual cases and their facts, it may also be viewed as in some sense forensic (see, for example, Connor 2008, p. 42; Schinkel 2008, p. 4).[15] As a matter of fact, the content of external and internal economic analyses should be identical.

---

[14] It should be added that the services provided by the said industry include not only actual testifying but also economic analyses supporting an argument that the party wants to make within an enforcement proceeding (Mandel 1999, p. 114) or informing compliance (Schinkel 2008, pp. 9–10).

[15] Compare this, for instance, with FBI's scientists involved in crime investigation and prosecution, whose work is also considered forensic even though they are employed by the government.

If we think, for example, about the market power of a business, it is supposed to be determined in the same way whether it is carried out by an expert witness or a public official. On the other hand, the two types of analyses may differ with respect to the procedural rules governing their integration into the decision-making process. Namely, submission of an expert opinion proffered by an outside expert will often be more heavily regulated than an analysis executed by an internal employee, which may nevertheless still face significant procedural constraints.

6.6   CONCLUSION

Forensic economics is economics informing any enforcement stage in any field of law, particularly through analyses of the facts of the case. As such, it is strongly constrained by applicable substantive and remedial legal rules, which it takes as given. Another set of constraints is imposed by rules of procedure, including rules of evidence. Economics-based analyses of case facts may be carried out by expert witnesses external to the enforcement body as well as by internal public officials. Forensic economics also has an academic branch, which addresses the question as to how to perform practical analyses.

REFERENCES

Aubuchon, Gregory. 2009. A Forensic Economist's Guide to Reading Legal Decisions. *Journal of Legal Economics* 16 (1): 71–82.
Blair, Roger D., and D. Daniel Sokol. 2015. Introduction. In *The Oxford Handbook of International Antitrust Economics*, ed. Roger D. Blair and D. Daniel Sokol, xiii. Oxford: Oxford University Press.
Breyer, Stephen. 1983. Economics for Lawyers and Judges. *Journal of Legal Education* 33 (2): 294–305.
Brookshire, Michael L. 1991. An Agenda for Future Research in Forensic Economics. *Journal of Forensic Economics* 4 (3): 287–296.
———. 2003. A History of the National Association of Forensic Economics, 1986–2001. *Litigation Economics Review* 6 (1): 22–32.
Brookshire, Michael L., Frank L. Slesnick, and Robert Lessne. 1990. The Emerging Industry of Forensic Economics: A Survey of NAFE Members. *Journal of Forensic Economics* 3 (2): 15–29.
Brunt, Maureen. 1999. Antitrust in the Courts: The Role of Economics and of Economists. In *International Antitrust Law & Policy: Fordham Corporate Law*

Institute Conference 1998, ed. Barry E. Hawk, 357–367. New York: Juris Publishing.

Canale, Damiano, and Giovanni Tuzet. 2020. What is Legal Reasoning About: A Jurisprudential Perspective. In *Economics in Legal Reasoning*, ed. Péter Cserne and Fabrizio Esposito, 9–24. London: Palgrave Macmillan.

Cappalli, Richard B. 2002. Bringing Internet Information to Court: Of "Legislative Facts". *Temple Law Review* 75 (1): 99–123.

Christiansen, Arndt, and Christian Ewald. 2014. Best Practices for Expert Economic Opinions—Key Element of Forensic Economics in Competition Law. In *Public and Private Enforcement of Competition Law in Europe*, ed. Kai Hüschelrath and Heike Schweitzer, 141–166. Berlin: Springer.

Connor, John M. 2008. Forensic Economics: An Introduction with Special Emphasis on Price Fixing. *Journal of Competition Law and Economics* 4 (1): 31–59.

Danziger, Leif, and Eliakim Katz. 2019. Compensation in Personal Injury Cases: Mean or Median Income? *European Journal of Law and Economics* 48 (2): 291–303.

Decker, Christopher. 2009. *Economics and the Enforcement of European Competition Law*. Cheltenham: Edward Elgar.

Dunoff, Jeffrey L., and Joel P. Trachtman. 1999. Economic Analysis of International Law. *Yale Journal of International Law* 24 (1): 1–59.

Eden, Philip, William B. Fairley, Curtis C. Aller, and C. Daniel Vencill. 1985. The Many Uses of Forensic Economics and Statistics. *Practical Lawyer* 31 (4): 25–36.

Fisher, Franklin M. 2008. Economic Analysis and "Bright-Line" Tests. *Journal of Competition Law and Economics* 4 (1): 129–153.

Froeb, Luke M., Paul A. Pautler, and Lars-Hendrik Röller. 2009. The Economics of Organizing Economists. *Antitrust Law Journal* 76 (2): 569–584.

Gavil, Andrew I. 2008. The Challenges of Economic Proof in a Decentralized and Privatized European Competition Policy System: Lessons from the American Experience. *Journal of Competition Law and Economics* 4 (1): 177–206.

Gerber, David J. 2009. Competition Law and the Institutional Embeddedness of Economics. In *Economic Theory and Competition Law*, ed. Josef Drexl, Laurence Idot, and Joël Monéger, 20–44. Cheltenham: Edward Elgar.

Giocoli, Nicola. 2020. Why US Judges Reject Economic Experts? In *Economics in Legal Reasoning*, ed. Péter Cserne and Fabrizio Esposito, 101–117. London: Palgrave Macmillan.

Hart, H.L.A. 1994. *The Concept of Law*. 2nd ed. Oxford: Clarendon Press.

Hart, Henry M., and Albert M. Sacks. 1994. *The Legal Process: Basic Problems in the Making and Application of Law*. Westbury, NY: The Foundation Press.

Hovenkamp, Herbert. 2005. *Antitrust Enterprise: Principle and Execution*. Cambridge, MA: Harvard University Press.

———. 2017. Economic Experts in Antitrust Cases. In *Modern Scientific Evidence: The Law and Science of Expert Testimony*, ed. David L. Faigman, Edward K. Cheng, Jennifer L. Mnookin, Erin E. Murphy, Joseph Sanders, and Christopher Slobogin, 965–1029. Eagan, MN: Thomson Reuters.

Hubková, Pavlína. 2020. Economics in Judicial Decision-Making: Four Types of Situations Where Judges May Apply Economics. In *Economics in Legal Reasoning*, ed. Péter Cserne and Fabrizio Esposito, 45–61. London: Palgrave Macmillan.

Ireland, Thomas R. 1997. The Interface between Law and Economics and Forensic Economics. *Journal of Legal Economics* 7 (1): 60–70.

———. 2016. Understanding Law as a Part of Forensic Economic Practice. In *Forensic Economics: Assessing Personal Damages in Civil Litigation*, ed. Frank D. Tinari, 261–277. New York: Palgrave Macmillan.

Jaffe, Louis L. 1955. Judicial Review: Question of Law. *Harvard Law Review* 69 (2): 239–276.

Jasanoff, Sheila. 2005. Law's Knowledge: Science for Justice in Legal Settings. *American Journal of Public Health* 95 (S1): S49–S58.

Klevorick, Alvin K. 1975. Law and Economic Theory: An Economist's View. *American Economic Review* 65 (2): 237–243.

Kovacic, William E., and David A. Hyman. 2012. Competition Agency Design: What's on the Menu? *European Competition Journal* 8 (3): 527–538.

Landes, William M., and Richard A. Posner. 1994. The Economics of Anticipatory Adjudication. *Journal of Legal Studies* 23 (2): 683–719.

Lanneau, Régis. 2014. To What Extent is the Opposition between Civil Law and Common Law Relevant for Law and Economics? In *Law and Economics in Europe: Foundations and Applications*, ed. Klaus Mathis, 23–46. Dordrecht: Springer.

Lianos, Ioannis. 2010. 'Judging' Economists: Economic Expertise in Competition Law Litigation: A European View. In *The Reform of EC Competition Law: New Challenges*, ed. Ioannis Lianos and Ioannis Kokkoris, 185–321. Alphen aan den Rijn: Kluwer Law International.

———. 2012. The Emergence of Forensic Economics in Competition Law: Foundations for a Sociological Analysis. *CLES Working Paper*, No. 5.

Lianos, Ioannis, and Christos Genakos. 2013. Econometric Evidence in EU Competition Law: An Empirical and Theoretical Analysis. In *Handbook on European Competition Law: Enforcement and Procedure*, ed. Ioannis Lianos and Damien Geradin, 1–137. Cheltenham: Edward Elgar.

Mandel, Michael J. 1999. Going for the Gold: Economists as Expert Witnesses. *Journal of Economic Perspectives* 13 (2): 113–120.

Padilla, A. Jorge. 2015. Fundamentos Económicos del Derecho de la Competencia en la UE: De la Reforma 'Monti' al Paquete de Modernización de las Ayudas de Estado. *Papeles de Economía Española* (145): 57–70.

Rodgers, James D., and Marc A. Weinstein. 2014. An Updated History of the National Association of Forensic Economics: 2002–2014. *Journal of Forensic Economics* 25 (2): 175–202.

Röller, Lars-Hendrik. 2005. Economic Analysis and Competition Policy Enforcement in Europe. In *Modelling European Mergers Theory, Competition Policy and Case Studies*, ed. Peter A.G. van Bergeijk, Erik Kloosterhuis, and Simon Bremer, 11–24. Cheltenham: Edward Elgar.

Schap, David. 2010a. Forensic Economics: An Overview. *Eastern Economic Journal* 36 (3): 347–352.

———. 2010b. Introduction to the Symposium on Forensic Economics. *Eastern Economic Journal* 36 (3): 344–346.

Schauer, Frederick. 1985. Easy Cases. *Southern California Law Review* 58 (2): 399–440.

Schinkel, Maarten Pieter. 2008. Forensic Economics in Competition Law Enforcement. *Journal of Competition Law and Economics* 4 (1): 1–30.

Sibony, Anne-Lise. 2012. Limits of Imports from Economics into Competition Law. In *The Global Limits of Competition Law*, ed. Ioannis Lianos and D. Daniel Sokol, 39–53. Stanford: Stanford University Press.

Stephenson, Stanley P., and David A. Macpherson. 2019. *Determining Economic Damages*. Costa Mesa: James Publishing.

Stigler, George J. 1992. Law or Economics? *Journal of Law and Economics* 35 (2): 455–468.

Thornton, Robert J., and John O. Ward. 1999. The Economist in Tort Litigation. *Journal of Economic Perspectives* 13 (2): 101–112.

Tinari, Frank D. 2010. The Practice of Forensic Economics: An Introduction. *Eastern Economic Journal* 36 (3): 398–406.

———., ed. 2016a. *Forensic Economics: Assessing Personal Damages in Civil Litigation*. New York: Palgrave Macmillan.

———. 2016b. An Introduction to the Field of Forensic Economics. In *Forensic Economics: Assessing Personal Damages in Civil Litigation*, ed. Frank D. Tinari, 1–16. New York: Palgrave Macmillan.

Ward, John O. 2014. The *Journal of Forensic Economics*: Revisiting Its Perspective and Agenda for Research. *Journal of Forensic Economics* 25 (1): 5–16.

Ward, John O., and Gerald W. Olson. 1987. Forensic Economics: A Perspective and An Agenda for Research. *Journal of Forensic Economics* 1 (1): 1–10.

Zitzewitz, Eric. 2012. Forensic Economics. *Journal of Economic Literature* 50 (3): 731–769.

CHAPTER 7

Why Do US Judges Reject Antitrust Experts?

Nicola Giocoli

Abstract Economists regularly appear as expert witnesses in antitrust litigations. The chapter analyzes how their models and methodologies have performed vis-à-vis the standards of relevance and reliability affirmed by the *US Supreme Court in Daubert v. Merrell Dow Pharm. Inc.* (1993). New data are provided on the number of antitrust economists whose expert testimonies have not survived a Daubert challenge. Explanations for such a poor record range from the judges' insufficient economic literacy to skewed procedural rules, from the high specificity of antitrust cases to widespread identification problems in economic models.

Keywords Antitrust • Daubert • Economists as experts • Identification problem • Judges' economic literacy

This chapter is a shortened version of Giocoli (2020). I thank the *Journal of the History of Economic Thought* for permission to republish some portions of it.

N. Giocoli (✉)
University of Pisa, Pisa, Italy
e-mail: nicola.giocoli@unipi.it

© The Author(s) 2020   101
P. Cserne, F. Esposito (eds.), *Economics in Legal Reasoning*,
Palgrave Studies in Institutions, Economics and Law,
https://doi.org/10.1007/978-3-030-40168-9_7

7.1   THE *DAUBERT* DOCTRINE

The Federal Rules of Evidence (FRE) govern the admission of evidence in US federal courts. When evidence consists of expert testimony, admission is policed by FRE 702—Testimony by Expert Witness. Unlike other witnesses, expert testimony is admissible without preliminary evidence (say, personal knowledge of the facts) showing the testimony's authenticity and relevance. To justify this deference to expert knowledge, courts need a clear definition of who is an expert. FRE 702 states that expert testimony is admissible if given by a witness who is "qualified as an expert by knowledge, skill, experience, training, or education", and if it is both "reliable" and "relevant" to the facts of the case.[1] The rule was revised in 2000 to reflect the standard articulated by the Supreme Court in a series of decisions taken between 1993 and 1999, starting with *Daubert v. Merrell Dow Pharm. Inc.*, 509 US 579 (1993).

By equating "reliable" to "scientific", the *Daubert* decision directed courts' attention to whether expert testimony is, or is not, science. Since 1993, it has therefore been up to judges to ensure not only that expert testimony is sufficiently tied to the facts of the case (relevance), but also that the methodology underlying the testimony is valid science (reliability). In legal jargon, *Daubert* and the ensuing FRE 702 have assigned judges the role of *gatekeepers* for the admission of scientific experts—a role they must perform by identifying what is relevant evidence and, above all, what is scientifically valid, and thus reliable, testimony.

While expressly avoiding establishing any "definitive checklist or test", the *Daubert* opinion pointed at some key factors for judges to consider in their gatekeeping function. The four so-called *Daubert criteria* to be checked are (1) whether the expert's methodology can or has been tested; (2) whether it has been subject to peer review and publication; (3) whether the employed scientific technique has a known or potential error rate or whether it admits standards controlling its operation; and (4) whether the methodology has attracted widespread acceptance within the relevant

---

[1] *Rule 702—Testimony by Expert Witnesses:* "A witness who is qualified as an expert by knowledge, skill, experience, training, or education may testify in the form of an opinion or otherwise if: (a) the expert's scientific, technical, or other specialized knowledge will help the trier of fact to understand the evidence or to determine a fact in issue; (b) the testimony is based on sufficient facts or data; (c) the testimony is the product of reliable principles and methods; and (d) the expert has reliably applied the principles and methods to the facts of the case."

scientific community (*Daubert*, at 593–594). These criteria, and the gate-keeping function itself, have triggered intense academic debate[2] and, more importantly, changed the way expert testimony is proffered in courts.

With *Daubert* the Supreme Court wanted to make sure juries be presented only with serious scientific evidence, rather than with so-called junk science (which could easily, though falsely, impress untrained jurors). The legal grounds for, as well as the practical advisability of, the new doctrine is thus beyond question: baseless testimony by unqualified witnesses should never be presented to a jury. Moreover, the judge's intervention should just guarantee that expert testimony has the proper methodological grounding and fit with the facts to be admissible; the determination of which of the (possibly multiple and contrasting) admitted expert testimony is correct—that is, the evaluation of the merit of the case—still rests with the jury.

As a matter of fact, however, *Daubert* has added an important weapon to litigation strategies. Raising a so-called *Daubert* challenge has become an oft-used option, with momentous consequences. A party may ask the court to assess the admissibility of the opposing party's expert witnesses, with the goal of excluding them at a preliminary stage. If successful, the challenge may strike a decisive blow to a party's chances, especially when the outcome of the case depends on technical or scientific matters.

Some kinds of experts are more exposed than others to *Daubert* challenges, though. This is, for instance, the case of expert economic testimony in antitrust litigations. The outcome has often been shocking. Several economists, including big names of the discipline, and even a few Nobel laureates, have seen their testimony rejected—in full or in part—by federal courts, following their failure to meet the *Daubert* standard of relevance and reliability. Indeed, data show that antitrust economists testifying for the plaintiff have approximately a one-in-two chance that at least part of their opinion will be excluded—an abnormal percentage in comparison to other disciplines, including other areas within economics. What is it in antitrust cases that makes the bar rise further, often to unreachable levels? Why is antitrust economics so exposed to *Daubert* challenges? The following pages suggest some explanations.

---

[2] The debate has involved philosophers of science, epistemologists, sociologists, and legal scholars. For more details and a few references, see Giocoli (2020).

7.2   ECONOMICS AND THE *DAUBERT* CRITERIA

It is under the legal framework of *Daubert* and FRE 702 that American judges are called to evaluate the relevance and reliability of expert economic testimony. The question arises as to whether experts in a social science like economics should be held to the same standards as experts in the natural sciences. Or should the bar be set differently? Questionable as they may be, the four *Daubert* criteria frame reliability assessments for expert testimony in the hard sciences, like laboratory physics or chemistry. But what about "soft" sciences, like social science in general, and economics in particular? In a later decision, *Kumho Tire Co. v. Carmichael* (526 U.S. 137, 1999), the Court explained that the standards of relevance and reliability apply to any kind of "scientific, technical or other specialized knowledge" (so FRE 702 now recites) proffered in expert testimony, but also that the *Daubert* criteria are neither necessary nor exhaustive.

Yet, the *Kumho* Court left unspecified in what cases—that is, for what type of expert knowledge—those criteria are more or less binding. On the one hand, their application to economics seems straightforward: economists too claim to proceed by the development of new theories and the generation of testable hypotheses. On the other, the kind of empirical testing of those very hypotheses that is typical of economics does not fully match the first criterion. Save for the still circumscribed area of experimental economics, testing in economics means comparing a theory's predictions against real-world observations, rather than against experimental data generated under controlled conditions.[3] So-called natural experiments may work nicely, yet they are not what the *Daubert* Court required; ditto for applied techniques based on data mining and story-building. The point is not only methodological, but practical. In the highly competitive realm of court litigation, the difference between the falsification standard envisioned by the Supreme Court and the actual methods of applied economics may be large enough to warrant exclusion of an expert economist's testimony.

The mismatch extends to the other *Daubert* criteria as well. As Bronsteen and Varma (2001, p. 14) put it, "[s]ome sound economic analyses may not be empirically testable or have a known or measurable error; some sound economic analyses may not be of sufficient interest to merit publication or peer review; and some sound economic analyses may be too

---

[3] Economists use to call it the identification problem. See Sect. 7.5.

esoteric to have attracted widespread acceptance within the relevant scientific community". In all these circumstances, the very sound economic analyses would not be admitted in court under a strict reading of the *Daubert* criteria. That testimony considered "professional" by academic economists may not be appropriate for litigation entails that the standard set by *Daubert* is higher than—or at least different from—that required for publication in professional journals.

A solution might be admitting that the *Daubert* criteria, with their explicit reference to the methodology of the natural sciences, are not applicable to a social science like economics. An economist's testimony should never be rejected under the falsifiability standard, for the simple reason that economics partakes more of "technical or specialized" knowledge, where such a standard does not apply, than of truly "scientific" knowledge—in short, that economists are more like the car tire experts in *Kumho Tire* than the biologists in *Daubert*. Alas, this way out would clash with the self-constructed image of "true scientists" economists have strived to build for decades in the eyes of the public opinion.

The troubled relationship between *Daubert* and economics culminates in antitrust cases. This is somehow ironic, given that industrial organization (IO) is the field where real experiments in economics were actually born[4] and that a specific subfield exists called forensic IO, allegedly supporting, both theoretically and empirically, all stages of competition law enforcement (see Schinkel 2008; Broulík 2020). Yet, data show that neither tradition nor self-esteem may save antitrust economists from falling more often than most other experts under the *Daubert* axe. For reasons examined in the following pages, the economic argument underlying antitrust testimonies frequently contains features that make it weak against a *Daubert* challenge—especially when the challenge comes from the defendant.

7.3 Tracking *Daubert* Challenges in Antitrust Cases

The frequent use of expert economic opinion, fears of unreliable expert testimony, and lawyers' strategic incentives have combined to make *Daubert* challenges a regular feature in antitrust litigations.

The first element is obvious. Economics expertise is indispensable in modern antitrust enforcement. Since the late 1970s, progress in IO and,

---

[4] See the surveys by Holt (1995) and Brandts and Potter (2018).

specifically, the Supreme Court's endorsement of a welfare-oriented approach have shifted antitrust analysis away from per se prohibitions toward an effects-based case-by-case approach.[5] Courts are required to determine which business behaviors are really anticompetitive—an assessment entailing complex factual issues: What is the relevant market? Does the defendant possess market power? Are the defendant's actions legitimate profit-seeking or an anticompetitive exercise of such power? The plaintiff has first to establish a coherent theory of anticompetitive effects and then assemble sufficient evidence to support the theory and overcome the defendant's efforts to defeat it. Hence, both parties make recourse to economic analysis and, consequently, to expert economic testimony.

Save for the aforementioned doubts about the four criteria's applicability, extending the *Daubert* doctrine to economics seems plain. Expert economic testimony is admissible if and only if (1) the witness is an expert in relevant aspects of economics, (2) the testimony is well grounded in those aspects of economics, and (3) the testimony applies the tools of economics to the facts of the case. In the spirit of *Daubert* and FRE 702, these principles should allow courts to get rid of "junk economics". Like other scientists, economists should thus welcome *Daubert*.

However, rules with commendable goals may have unintended consequences. When applied to antitrust cases, *Daubert*'s impact has gone beyond its expected deterrent effect on irrelevant or unreliable testimony. It is even questionable whether its application has really protected antitrust juries from "junk economics". On the one side, *Daubert* rulings have *de facto* replaced the jury with the judge as the finder of facts who weighs opposing expert evidence. On the other, and precisely because of the key role expert economic testimony plays in antitrust litigations, *Daubert* challenges have become a customary defense strategy, whose success is independent of the merit of the case, that is, the alleged antitrust violation,[6] and sometimes even of the proffered testimony's intrinsic quality, as certified by the "general acceptance" that the given theory of the violation may have in top-notch IO literature.

Available data validate the latter claim. Although *Daubert* equally applies to plaintiffs' and defendants' experts, an analysis by James Langenfeld and Christopher Alexander of more than 400 *Daubert* motions

---

[5] See Gavil (2000, p. 835), Solow and Fletcher (2006, p. 489), and Baye and Wright (2011, pp. 2–3).
[6] For prescient remarks, see Gavil (2001, p. 6).

lodged against economic experts suggested that *Daubert* has created an additional barrier to plaintiffs' successful assertion of antitrust claims (Langenfeld and Alexander 2011). A few regularities emerged.

First, economists appeared to be challenged more frequently in antitrust cases than in all other legal areas (like intellectual property, product liability, or securities) where they are summoned as expert witnesses.[7] Second, while *Daubert* challenges of economic experts had a fair chance of succeeding in all legal areas, Langenfeld and Alexander's data showed that economists were much more likely to be excluded when testifying on antitrust matters. Third, confirming that *Daubert* challenges had become a routine litigation tool for antitrust defendants, plaintiffs' experts were more likely to be challenged than defendants' experts: according to Langenfeld and Alexander, more than 80% of *Daubert* challenges in antitrust cases attacked plaintiffs' experts. Fourth, a much greater chance existed in antitrust cases of excluding plaintiffs' economic experts as compared to defendants' experts. Indeed, Langenfeld and Alexander showed that almost 50% of challenges against plaintiffs' economic experts succeeded, in all or in part. Even notable economists could be excluded when acting as plaintiff's witnesses, such as leading industrial economists Franklin Fisher and Richard Schmalensee, American Economic Association President Robert Hall, and Nobel Prize winner Robert Lucas. In contrast, antitrust plaintiffs had been less effective in excluding economists supporting the defendant. Those numbers thus confirmed that, by 2011, *Daubert* had created a new, disproportionate burden on plaintiffs bringing antitrust claims.

Courtesy of *Daubert Tracker*, an online paid service providing litigants with the broadest database of *Daubert* challenges divided by subjects, we can update Langenfeld and Alexander's numbers.[8] The outcomes are the same—possibly worse. Between 2012 and 2018, 4550 *Daubert* challenges have been raised, in US Federal Courts and in all areas of the law, against expert testimony on the subjects of economics and finance. For comparison, only 2109 such challenges have been raised against expert testimony on DNA analysis and forensic science in the same period. Overall, since

---

[7] According to Langenfeld and Alexander (2011, p. 23 and Table 1), roughly one fifth of *Daubert* challenges against economists came in antitrust cases, despite the latter representing only 0.3% of total cases between 2000 and 2008.

[8] See www.dauberttracker.com. I am especially grateful to *Daubert Tracker* CEO Myles Levin for having granted free access to the database. The following analysis also used *LexisNexis*.

1993, economics and finance together rank fourth (behind only medicine, engineering, and psychology, and above usual suspects, such as police enforcement and law itself) among the areas of expertise most often challenged under *Daubert*.

As to antitrust law, 971 cases have been litigated in US Federal courts between 2012 and 2018. Among them, an astounding 886 *Daubert*-related challenges have been raised against all areas of expertise. Of these, 584 challenges attacked economics expert witnesses. Even considering that almost always more than one expert is called to testify and that multiple *Daubert* challenges may be raised in a single case, the numbers are impressive. Again for comparison, consider that, within a universe of more than 3000 cases for each area of the law, economists have been challenged only 254 times when providing testimony on securities and finance law and 371 times as experts on patent and copyright law. Under the safe assumption that parties in litigation are more likely to raise a *Daubert* challenge against testimonies whose relevance and reliability looks *a priori* questionable, the picture emerging from these data is as dismal for expert economic witnesses in antitrust cases as that depicted by Langenfeld and Alexander in 2011.

In line again with Langenfeld and Alexander's remark about the higher frequency of challenges against economic experts for the plaintiff, roughly two thirds of the 584 challenges raised in antitrust cases between 2012 and 2018 attacked plaintiff experts (391 out of 584). Of the remaining, 192 targeted experts for the defendant and 1 a (rare instance of) court-appointed expert. Slightly less than half of those challenges were successful in either partially or fully excluding expert economic testimony from being presented to the court: 269 out of 584 (46%). Of these, 155 (40%) succeeded against plaintiff experts and 114 (59%) against defendant experts.[9]

The list of big names in economics or, more specifically, IO struck down under *Daubert* has also lengthened since 2012. According to *Daubert Tracker*, expert testimony by the likes of Douglas Bernheim, Timothy Bresnahan, Dennis Carlton, James Heckman, Janusz Ordover, Daniel Rubinfield, Robert Willig, Orley Ashenfelter, Daniel McFadden, Carl Shapiro, and Joe Stiglitz has been either partially or totally excluded in an antitrust case following a successful *Daubert* challenge. Courts have partially or totally dismissed those testimonies, as well as many others by

---

[9] This figure (59% of success against defendant experts) is the only significant difference with respect to Langenfeld and Alexander's findings.

scores of professional economists, as either irrelevant or unreliable, or both. Hence, antitrust experts are still especially likely to fall under the *Daubert* axe. Why?

Part of the evidence, like the greater propensity of antitrust defendants to challenge the admissibility of economic testimony, has straightforward explanation. Plaintiffs have the burden of proof in antitrust cases and, as we said, economics plays an essential part in it. "In order to win", Langenfeld and Alexander (2011, p. 21) explained, "plaintiffs may need to wade into complicated economic waters to establish the necessary elements of their claims, such as relevant market, market power, and antitrust injury". An antitrust complaint may thus founder even before the beginning of the trial if deprived of the expert economist's testimony supporting it. The converse is not true for antitrust defendants, whose task is often just to demolish the plaintiff's argument—a task that may in principle be carried on even without specific economic expertise. In short, the incentives for raising a *Daubert* challenge are much stronger for antitrust defendants than for plaintiffs.

Other parts are, however, harder to explain. The commonest reason for exclusion of economic testimony is lack of reliability, which in turn stems from the inadequate methodology used by the expert (or the insufficiency of the data, given the methodology). Consider again the four *Daubert* criteria and their implied characterization of "valid science". The consensus is that expert economic testimony should partake of such a characterization because economics *is* "valid science" (whatever this may mean). The latter belief is crucial to the image most economists—above all, applied ones like those providing testimony in antitrust litigations—have self-constructed of their own profession. Alas, differently from other sciences, the methodological blueprint of antitrust economics shows a poor fit with the notion of "valid science" embodied by the *Daubert* criteria. Antitrust cases thus become a trap into which even the best economic minds may fall.

7.4 WHY THE *DAUBERT* SYNDROME?

The simplest answer is that economists are right and courts are wrong—in other words, courts fall short of the task assigned them by *Daubert* for want of economic knowledge. How can judges assess the validity of an expert's methodology? Worse, how can they assess whether the expert's opinion fits the facts of the case? Yet, this is what they are called to do when, as it often happens in antitrust cases, the appraisal of broad methodological principles blurs into the even more difficult evaluation of how the expert's methodology handles the available evidence. Add that no court should be called to "resolve disputes among respected, well credentialed scientists about matters squarely within their expertise, in areas where there is no scientific consensus".[10] If asked to do so, especially in highly technical matters like antitrust complaints, courts will likely make bad calls and fail to properly grasp economic science, possibly dismissing valid expert testimonies by "well credentialed" economists.

While this answer contains more than a grain of truth, the true meaning of *Daubert* and FRE 702 should not be misunderstood. No court is compelled to resolve scientific disputes among experts, or to replace the jury as fact finder. The *Daubert* criteria aim precisely at avoiding such difficult calls, by allowing all kinds of expert testimony that may be deemed scientific, to the sole exclusion of unscientific ones. As Werden (2008, p. 817) underlines, the spirit and the letter of *Daubert* is that the deficiencies that should lead a court to exclude an expert testimony on, say, economics should be identifiable *without* any specific expertise in economics. This optimistic view must, however, be weighed *vis-à-vis* the reality of modern antitrust litigation, where complex economic (and statistical) analysis is the bread and butter of every expert testimony. It defies credulity to believe that such complexity may have no impact on judicial decision-making. Indeed, antitrust decisions are often criticized because of the judges' misunderstanding of the relevant economics, of their failure to recognize the true economic issue, or of their reliance on the analysis of the wrong expert.[11]

Specific claims that the federal judiciary is not equipped to competently evaluate complex economic evidence in antitrust cases have been seldom subjected to empirical validation. The best such effort so far[12] was undertaken some years ago by the Antitrust Section of the American Bar Association (ABA), which assembled a task force of leading economists and lawyers, plus a federal judge, to study the role of economic evidence

---

[10] This is what the Ninth Circuit Court lamented in *Daubert v. Merrell Dow Pharms.*, 43 F.3d 1311, 1316 (9th Cir. 1995), quoted by Werden (2008, p. 817).

[11] The Supreme Court itself has acknowledged the almost insurmountable challenges that the economic analysis of antitrust issues presents to generalist judges and juries. See, for example, *Bell Atl. Corp. v. Twombly*, 550 U.S. 544, 2007, at 558–559.

[12] For another exception, see Baye and Wright (2011), who attempt to examine the effects of economic complexity and basic economic training on judicial decisions in antitrust cases.

in federal courts. The ABA report concluded that lack of proper economic understanding "can seriously affect the adversarial process by skewing judicial outcomes, by leading decision makers to ignore conflicting economic testimony or come to 'wrong' conclusions, and can increase litigation costs" (Baker and Morse 2006, p. 2). Only less than a quarter of the 42 antitrust economists interviewed by the task force believed that judges "usually" understand the economic issues in an antitrust case (ibid., App. II, p. 2).

An alternative, and somehow complementary, answer explains the poor record of antitrust economists against *Daubert* with the workings of the legal system. Ideally, antitrust complaints should be drafted by plaintiffs' attorneys after consultation with an economist. What happens in reality, note Solow and Fletcher (2006, p. 495), is that the expert economist comes into play only at a second stage, after the complaint has been presented. Hence, the economist is constrained to work within the theory offered in the complaint and with the data the plaintiff has been able to obtain through discovery. Upon taking on the case, the economist cannot turn to whatever market provides data from which to draw conclusions, as she would do in her academic activity, but has to work only with the evidence available in the case at hand. Life is easier for the defendant's expert, who by legal rules has the advantage of responding to the claims made by the plaintiff's economist, and so may just focus on criticizing the opposing expert's opinion.

This asymmetry imposed by legal rules mixes up with the (debatable) epistemology underlying the *Daubert* doctrine to generate a tricky situation. It has been noted that the Supreme Court's reading of the crucial "is it reliable?" question fits nicely with the requirements of legal analysis, but much less so with those of economic theory (Coate and Fischer 2012, pp. 140–141). The first *Daubert* criterion raises an absolute question—can the alleged scientific testimony be falsified?—which only admits a dichotomic, yes-or-no answer. The Court's purely instrumental appeal to (naive) falsificationism as a tool allowing scientists to discard theories was tailor-made for courtroom use, because it reduced the analysis of an expert testimony to a specific question. Indeed, this is what courts normally look for, namely, straightforward decision-making tools, more than realistic explanations or elegant deductive chains.

What makes the mix between skewed procedural rules and amateurish epistemology dangerous is then a matter of incentives. As early as 1999, in a short essay tellingly titled "Going for the Gold", Michael Mandel complained about the risks of the economists' "booming expert business". "Economists would be the first to agree that large-scale monetary incentives can change behavior", he wrote (Mandel 1999, p. 113). When serving as expert witness, the economist is no truth-seeker anymore, but becomes part of a legal process, whose logic is "adversarial, rather than scientific" and where "lawyers are calling the shots" (ibid., p. 117). The combination of hefty fees and the dominant role of lawyers changes the nature of the economics being done by the expert: legal success only matters, not the best economic understanding. In an adversarial game the rules are not those of academic publication. The yes-or-no question implicit in any *Daubert* challenge, when combined with the economist's urge to make the case for the party paying her/him, and with the *de jure* comparative weakness of the plaintiff's position, may expose a testimony's methodological frailties to the point of making it unacceptable under the *Daubert* standard.

One last immediate reason for the high rate of successful *Daubert* challenges in antitrust jurisprudence calls into play the specificity of antitrust cases. No economist—not even a Nobel Laureate—is qualified to testify about every economic issue that may arise in antitrust litigation. It is not just that even the best economic minds may not have enough experience on the particular issues and specific analytical methods of a given case. IO specialists are obviously qualified to testify on most issues arising in antitrust cases; still, IO expertise is neither necessary nor sufficient to save an economist from a *Daubert* challenge. Even a highly respected IO economist may be unqualified to testify on basic issues in a specific case. As we know, FRE 702 requires that expert testimony be "based upon sufficient facts or data". In antitrust the proviso is often interpreted as requiring that the testimony be grounded in the facts of the given industry relevant for the given case. Generally speaking, an economist with no research record in the particular industry or whose testimony incorporates few case- or industry-specific facts, but rather offers a "one size fits all" account, is more likely to suffer rejection under *Daubert*.[13]

This conclusion is shared by the best economic knowledge. "The application of reasonableness standards in antitrust decision-making and the

---

[13] A famous example is the exclusion by the trial court in *In re Brand Name Prescription Drugs Antitrust Litig.*, (1999-1 Trade Cas. (CCH) 72, 446, N.D. Ill.) of most of the testimony proffered for the plaintiff by Nobel laureate Robert Lucas. According to the court, Lucas had inadequate knowledge of the specific nature of the pharmaceutical industry.

modern empirical literature in industrial organization economics have an important commonality", write leading IO scholars Baker and Bresnahan (2008, p. 27). "[B]oth treat the industry as the appropriate unit of observation. Both fields recognize that a one-size-fits-all approach to analyzing business conduct won't do, since so much variation in outcomes arises from factors specific to each individual industry." Again, a key asymmetry between plaintiff and defendant is also at play here: "little or no factual foundation may be required for economic testimony that merely critiques the analysis of another economic expert, because errors or gaps in economic logic may be clear without any knowledge of the particular facts of a case" (Werden 2008, p. 810). How many of the casualties of a *Daubert* challenge were economists providing a generic, nonindustry-based testimony on behalf of the plaintiff?[14]

7.5 ANTITRUST ECONOMICS'S SPECIAL WEAKNESS

The previous section offered a few reasons for the unusual frequency and success rate of *Daubert* challenges in antitrust cases. The judges' insufficient familiarity with economic methods, the procedural peculiarities of the legal system, and the less-than-encyclopedic factual experience of even the smartest economist combine to produce a not-so-favorable environment for economic experts. Still, these features seem hardly specific to antitrust and could work for economic testimony in other areas of the law, such as product liability. The data on *Daubert* challenges suggest otherwise. Something else seems to affect economic expertise when summoned in antitrust cases. This section examines whether anything special exists with the way economic analysis is applied to antitrust that justifies the higher exposure to *Daubert* attacks of economic testimony for the plaintiff.[15]

Antitrust cases are *theory-driven*: even when formally dealing with questions of fact, it is the economic theory endorsed by the court that governs the legality of the business practice at issue. This is because antitrust laws, such as the Sherman Act and Clayton Act, have no self-evident meaning.

---

[14] Answering this question would require an analysis of the specific, case-by-case motivations for the rejection—something which transcends the limits of the present chapter.

[15] For reasons of space we will not deal with another possible explanation, which calls into play the methodological distance separating the approach to IO that, inspired by the Chicago School, still dominates antitrust enforcement in America, from that considered mainstream by most academic literature, the so-called Post-Chicago approach. See Giocoli (2020).

What these statutes mean requires the intermediation of a theoretical construct that interprets their vague general principles in terms of the specific situation. Consider, for instance, monopolization (Sherman Act, Sec. 2). In the nineteenth century, the term had a traditional, common law construction as synonymous of forestalling or engrossing. When the Sherman Act pushed courts to find a new meaning for it, it was quickly acknowledged that the notion only makes sense in terms of a market that the indicted business is allegedly monopolizing. But "a market" is, in turn, a purely theoretical construct, that is, a notion that only makes sense in antitrust enforcement through the mediation of an economic theory identifying it (by using, say, cross-elasticities or other techniques). More generally, any allegation of anticompetitive behavior must rely upon a (hopefully, properly specified) economic theory, as well as on a set of data supporting it. In short, there is no such thing as an a-theoretical antitrust allegation. Stand-alone data are of very little use to a court. The well-known distinction between correlation and causation is there to remind us that no empirical relationship between economic magnitudes can be interpreted without theoretical guidance. It is thus up to economic theory to suggest a potential causal chain that may account for the observed data and whose implications may be subjected to empirical validation.

Presenting the court with the theory upholding an antitrust allegation is the expert economist's task. In the post-*Daubert* world, the court is then asked to check the relevance and reliability of that economic argument. A conclusion may thus be tentatively drawn. Against Werden's optimistic claim (see previous section), the sheer number and high success rate of *Daubert* challenges against economic experts for the plaintiff are evidence of the questionable status of the economics underlying so many antitrust allegations—questionable, that is to say, to the legally trained eyes of the defendant's attorneys and the court.

The problem is indeed familiar to antitrust economists. Like most work in empirical social science, antitrust analysis makes inferences from evidence without the benefit of performing fully-fledged experiments. A distinctive issue thus arises called the *identification problem*. Economists must "look carefully for settings in which nature has created an experiment for them" and must "explain why it is reasonable to interpret the data as having been created by an implicit experiment, and describe the nature of that experiment" (Baker and Bresnahan 2008, p. 13). This explanation—called identification—is a crucial part of empirical economic analysis, in that it should clarify on which basis a given theory can be preferred to another for interpreting the available evidence. The identification problem has obvious relevance in antitrust, when juries—in their role of finder of facts—must select between alternative interpretations of the data. Yet, the problem may also affect the litigation at a preliminary stage, that of a *Daubert* challenge raised against the specific theory identified by the expert for the plaintiff to support the allegation.

Assume the expert economist has observed price and quantity data about the market under scrutiny and, on their basis, is offering an opinion about future prices. The first problem she faces—and the first possible way her testimony may be challenged under *Daubert*—is to select one among the many alternative models, each with different predictions about future prices, which can be parametrized with the available data. Remember that for any discipline that, like economics, reclaims scientific status, the *Daubert* criteria should help courts to determine "whether a theory or technique is scientific knowledge".

Let's assume then that, because of its ability to account for observed market data, the economist's theory passes the relevance check. Still, the reliability scrutiny may be troublesome. The four criteria for "valid science" are of little use here. In an antitrust case, the reliability issue cannot always be exhausted by checking for the falsifiability, peer validation, statistical accountability, and widespread acceptance of the proposed economic model or technique. The gatekeeping task compels the court to the more exacting scrutiny of whether that very model or technique is also appropriate for, and properly applied to, the specific case. It is at this junction that a major difference between economics and most other "scientifically valid" disciplines emerges.

Even Werden concedes that "economics has no well-established standards governing the selection and application of particular models and methods" (Werden 2008, p. 815)—which amounts to saying that a *Daubert* challenge necessarily brings an antitrust court to transcend the four criteria. Baker and Bresnahan (2008, p. 13) state the problem most clearly: "All antitrust cases that go to trial involve a contest between at least two distinct theories explaining firm conduct, one in which the challenged behavior lessens competition and one in which it is efficient." This is where the identification problem sets in, directing attention on the correspondence between the evidence and the competing economic theories, and thus on whether the evidence can be used to distinguish between competing theories of the case.

The point is not so much that economic experts present conflicting models of the same antitrust issue. These analyses may all rest on solid methodological grounds and, as we know, *Daubert* neither requires nor empowers courts to determine which of multiple competing scientific theories is the best. Nor that a divergence may exist about the facts themselves, contrasting versions of which may be offered by the parties. Again, FRE 702 is not intended to authorize the exclusion of an expert's testimony on the ground that the judge believes one version of the facts or another. The true point is *how to verify the reliability* of the economic (and often also statistical) theory supporting the interpretation of the facts.

For external observers like judges, the mere circumstance that economists strongly disagree with one another on many antitrust issues—and consequently offer widely divergent models to explain them—may suffice to destroy their testimonies' reliability. So drastic a view hinges on the fundamental idea that, while legal decision-making has at its core the rules for weighing one against the other conflicting interpretations of the same facts, *no such rules seem to exist in the case of antitrust economics*. This, by itself, may be read as evidence of the unreliability of economic models. The economists' failure to provide courts with a method to select between competing models of the same market phenomena may thus lead *Daubert* gatekeepers to discard most of the economics underlying antitrust complaints. In other words, the high success rate of *Daubert* challenges appears as the inevitable outcome of the intrinsic inability of a large chunk of antitrust economics to satisfy an essential requirement of legal analysis.

References

Baker, Jonathan B., and Timothy F. Bresnahan. 2008. Economic Evidence in Antitrust: Defining Markets and Measuring Market Power. In *Handbook of Antitrust Economics*, ed. Paolo Buccirossi, 1–42. Cambridge, MA: MIT Press.

Baker, Jonathan B., and M. Howard Morse. 2006. *Final Report of Economic Evidence Task Force*. American Bar Association. Accessed September 4, 2017. www.americanbar.org/content/dam/aba/migrated/antitrust/at-reports/01_c_ii.authcheckdam.pdf.

Baye, Michael R., and Joshua D. Wright. 2011. Is Antitrust Too Complicated for Generalist Judges? The Impact of Economic Complexity and Judicial Training on Appeals. *Journal of Law and Economics* 54: 1–24.

Brandts, Jordi, and Jan Potter. 2018. Experimental Industrial Organization. In *Handbook of Game Theory and Industrial Organization, Volume II. Applications*, ed. Luis C. Corchón and Marco A. Marini, 453–474. Cheltenham: Elgar.

Bronsteen, Peter, and Asim Varma. 2001. *Daubert* Rules of Economists. *Antitrust* 15: 14–16.

Broulík, Jan. 2020. What is Forensic Economics? In *Economics in Legal Reasoning*, ed. Péter Cserne and Fabrizio Esposito, 83–99. London: Palgrave Macmillan.

Coate, Malcolm B., and Jeffrey H. Fischer. 2012. *Daubert*, Science, and Modern Game Theory: Implications for Merger Analysis. *Supreme Court Economic Review* 20: 125–182.

Gavil, Andrew I. 2000. Defining Reliable Forensic Economics in the Post-*Daubert/Kumho Tire* Era: Case Studies from Antitrust. *Washington & Lee Law Review* 57: 831–878.

———. 2001. *Daubert* Comes of Age. *Antitrust* 15: 6.

Giocoli, Nicola. 2020. Rejected! Antitrust Economists as Expert Witnesses in the Post-*Daubert* world. *Journal of the History of Economic Thought* (forthcoming). https://doi.org/10.1017/S1053837219000671.

Holt, Charles A. 1995. Industrial Organization: A Survey of Laboratory Research. In *Handbook of Experimental Economics*, ed. John Kagel and Alvin E. Roth, 349–443. Princeton: Princeton UP.

Langenfeld, James, and Christopher Alexander. 2011. *Daubert* and Other Gatekeeping Challenges of Antitrust Experts. *Antitrust* 25: 21–28 and Appendix.

Mandel, Michael J. 1999. Going for the Gold: Economists as Expert Witnesses. *Journal of Economic Perspectives* 13: 113–120.

Schinkel, Maarten P. 2008. Forensic Economics in Competition Law Enforcement. *Journal of Competition Law and Economics* 4: 1–30.

Solow, John L., and Daniel Fletcher. 2006. Doing Good Economics in the Courtroom: Thoughts on *Daubert* and Expert Testimony in Antitrust. *Journal of Corporation Law* 31: 489–502.

Werden, Gregory J. 2008. The Admissibility of Expert Testimony. In *Issues in Competition Law and Policy*, vol. I, 801–817. American Bar Association—Section of Antitrust Law.

PART IV

New Perspectives

CHAPTER 8

Fostering the Autonomy of Legal Reasoning Through Legal Realism

Felipe Figueroa Zimmermann

Abstract This chapter explains why the dominant pattern of disciplinary interaction between law and economics has fostered a general trend of reducing legal reasoning to economic reasoning. After describing the pattern of interaction between both disciplines through the example of property rights (Sect. 8.2) and linking it to the debate on reductionism in philosophy of science (Sect. 8.3), the chapter proposes a strategy for salvaging the autonomy of legal reasoning by increasing reflexivity through a version of legal realism inspired by the work of Otto Neurath (Sect. 8.4).

Keywords Neoclassical economics • Formalism realism • Otto Neurath • Logical positivism • Reflexivity • Interdisciplinarity • Law and economics • Reductionism • Legal reasoning

F. Figueroa Zimmermann (✉)
University of Warwick, Coventry, UK
e-mail: f.figueroa-zimmermann@warwick.ac.uk

© The Author(s) 2020
P. Cserne, F. Esposito (eds.), *Economics in Legal Reasoning*,
Palgrave Studies in Institutions, Economics and Law,
https://doi.org/10.1007/978-3-030-40168-9_8

121

8.1   INTRODUCTION

The pattern of disciplinary interaction between law and economics is such that, as a response to the "expansive" and "reductionist" program of economists, legal theorists are forced to flesh out the normative considerations expressed in the systematic features that guide legal reasoning in the different branches of law. This trend is unstable, due to the defensive character of the legal theorists' argumentative strategy. Legal theorists' only answer to the advances of the economists is to try to refute them by proposing features of law and legal reasoning that cannot be reduced to economic terms. In this sense, the debate regarding disciplinary boundaries is closely related to a long-standing dispute in philosophy of science between reductionists and anti-reductionists. The reductionist argument is that theories of one discipline can be replaced, without losing any relevant knowledge, by the theories of another discipline. Conversely, anti-reductionists denounce that valuable insights are sacrificed in the process.

Alas, it is always possible to assert the insufficiency of legal scholars' anti-reductionist strategy by showing that the allegedly irreducible features are, after all, reducible to economic terms, or, alternatively, are irrelevant or pathologic. Whatever answer the economists choose, their claim to epistemic authority over legal phenomena can continue to increase as each attempt at carving out a safe space for autonomous legal reasoning is overcome. As this trend continues, it permeates the institutional organization of disciplines and eventually legal institutions.

The question for those interested in salvaging the autonomy of legal reasoning is how to alter this structural pattern of disciplinary interaction. This requires sustainable balance of epistemic authority between legal theory and economics that would have the benefit of increasing reflexivity in both disciplines. This chapter proposes a strategy for attaining this goal: rehabilitating legal realism. The aim should be to undermine economics' claims to superior accuracy regarding predictions and causal explanation. This requires legal theory to go beyond conceptual analysis, which would only mark the beginning of the enquiry rather than its end. In this sense, a rebalancing of epistemic authority between law and economics entails a rehabilitation of legal realism.

8.2   The Bundle Theory of Rights and the Interaction of Law and Economics

The economic analysis of law purports to show the expected effects of legal arrangements. The underlying idea is that economists' predictions can be empirically tested by anyone. Thus, their epistemic authority (allegedly) relies on the accuracy of the predictions, instead of the dominance of arcane technical language or ethical principles (as would be the case with legal scholars, lawyers and judges).

The approach's appeal is that the disciplines would compete for providing the best explanations for any given set of phenomena. This view sees disciplinary boundaries as monopoly-generating obstacles to knowledge: they are the result of what Bentham called the "sinister interests of Judge & Co" (Atria 2016, pp. 63–65), what is now called rent-seeking behavior by self-appointed and self-reproducing elites (Leeson 2019).

To regard current disciplinary boundaries as the "proper" domain of each discipline entails a positive judgment about the efficacy of the current organization of scientific disciplines. To put it bluntly, it involves a conservative attitude towards the status quo. Thus, regarding disciplinary boundaries as defining the proper domain of each discipline places the burden of proof on those who would have the current disciplinary boundaries altered or eliminated.[1] The opposite assessment is behind efforts to justify the erosion of disciplinary boundaries: the failure to do so entails a wasted opportunity. They are obstacles to knowledge and a necessary evil at best.

Thus, the case for an economic analysis of legal phenomena can be justified by the epistemic gains to be obtained by eroding disciplinary boundaries, so that no single approach should have a monopoly over a field. Contrariwise, the opposition to this approach can be justified by arguing that there are epistemic gains to be obtained by keeping disciplinary boundaries in place.

In the case of law and economics, one of the prime sites of interaction (and conflict) is property rights theory, where the disciplinary boundaries are thinner and the economists have made the most substantive contributions to legal theory. Thus, property rights theory provides an excellent

---

[1] It could be argued that this attitude is prevalent among philosophers of science: in their zeal to explain why science has been successful, they easily slip into assuming it has been as successful as it can be.

vantage point to investigate the pattern of disciplinary interaction of law and economics.

In this section, it will be argued that the theoretical assumptions built into the bundle theory of rights generate a strong theoretical bias toward using economics to study legal phenomena.[2] Consequently, its widespread adoption has entailed an encroachment of economics within domains that have been traditionally considered within the competence of jurisprudence. As a result, the autonomy of legal reasoning has been questioned. Legal theorists who oppose this trend argue—as their anti-reductionist counterparts in philosophy of science—that this has an epistemic cost: some normative considerations that are embedded in legal categories cannot be accounted for by economics. As the dominance of economics over law increases, these normative features are kept out of sight, until eventually they are no longer recognized as features of legal institutions.

As a result of Coase's overwhelming influence, the bundle theory of rights became a key element of the conceptual framework of contemporary mainstream law and economics (Merrill and Smith 2001). The bundle theory of rights has fostered a view stating that to any valuable attribute of an asset corresponds a use-right. Each of these use-rights can be held as property by an agent. Thus, they can also be traded through contracts. Furthermore, since all allocations of use-rights have economic effects (i.e. they entail distributional effects in wealth) (Commons 1924), there are no conceptual boundaries outside of which the framework of economics cannot be applied.

In sum, for legal scholars and economists using the bundle theory of rights, "property consists of nothing more than the authoritative list of permitted uses of a resource—posted, as it were, by the State for each object of scarcity" (Merrill and Smith 2001, p. 366). They assume as a theoretical framework a formalized market in which agents trade through the price system. Since all allocations of legal entitlements have economic effects, all of them are susceptible to economic analysis. This also means that every entitlement is in principle susceptible to being the object of a market transaction. Under this view, nothing remains outside the scope of economic expertise.

Another way in which the bundle theory of rights generates a bias toward the use of economics is that the content of a Hohfeldian claim-right is indeterminate without a conception of what counts as an

---

[2] Smith (2019) reaches the same conclusion via a different, but related, argument.

interference. What counts as an interference with an action cannot be discovered only by describing the action protected by the claim-right. This is because what counts as an interference depends on how interference is defined and not on the definition of the action which is the subject of that interference. The definition of an action leaves undetermined which of the alternative definitions of what counts as an interference should determine the content of the duty correlative to a claim right. Thus, a criterion for choosing such a notion is necessary for the bundle theory of rights to be operative. Such a criterion is provided by the notion of externality, that is, any event produced by an agent that alters another agent's cost structure in performing an action (Buchanan and Stubblebine 1962). In turn, the idea that externalities should be incorporated in the cost structure of those who generate them constitutes the benchmark under which the determination of Hohfeldian claim-rights can be evaluated: if rights are determined in this way and transaction costs are reduced, the resulting allocation of rights will approach efficiency (Mathis and Shannon 2009, chapter 4).

To sum up, the bundle theory of rights generates a bias toward the use of economics to explain legal institutions in at least two senses: first, all legal phenomena can be analyzed by using economics, since the allocation of legal entitlements always has economic consequences and all legal entitlements can be conceptualized as tradable assets. Second, the bundle theory of rights is not complete without a theory of interference, which is exactly what the notion of externality provides.

Consequently, as the use of the bundle theory of rights becomes more ubiquitous among legal scholars, the expertise of economists becomes increasingly necessary for understanding law.

The appeal of the mainstream law and economics view on the bundle theory of rights is that, by treating all existing things as usable resources, it puts into focus how agents use things to achieve different ends. It also privileges a view under which it is the agents' prerogative to dispose and use these things as they see fit. It does this in a straightforward fashion, focusing on the costs and benefits their use imposes on agents. It is this last feature that, according to its critics, constitutes its main shortcoming: this approach ignores (indeed, it must ignore) noninstrumental normative considerations that (as they claim) are embedded in legal categories: for example, notions such as wrongdoing and duty or the distinction between a sanction and a tax (Smith 2011). For economists, such noninstrumental normative considerations are at best superficial and unnecessary accoutrements to legal reasoning and at worse irrational distortions. On the contrary, thinking like a lawyer entails understanding legal categories and the normative consequences that derive from them. Thus, legal reasoning is reasoning through these categories. If one dismisses them, one has moved beyond the realm of law (Schauer 2009).

8.3   REDUCTIONISM AND ANTI-REDUCTIONISM IN LAW AND ECONOMICS

As shown in the previous section, the debate regarding what should be the relationship between law and economics has been carried out in terms of the question regarding the validity of legal categories vis-à-vis economic explanation. As was briefly mentioned in the introduction, this debate is analogous to a long-standing debate in philosophy of science: between reductionism and anti-reductionism. Finding a way out of this debate requires reframing it in a way that fleshes out clearly what is at stake in each position. This will be done via a distinction from legal philosophy, that is the distinction between the internal and the external point of view.

Nowadays, following the work of HLA Hart, contemporary analytical anglophone legal theory has tended to stress the importance of what he called the internal point of view. Thus, it is generally acknowledged that law can only be grasped from the standpoint of the agents involved in legal practice.

In the context of a still very much Hart-dominated legal culture, the attractiveness of having an external point of view to study legal systems (i.e. that the categories of legal reasoning are "reducible" to the concepts of another discipline such as economics) must be stated explicitly. One can only question the underlying or tacit assumptions that guide legal reasoning within a discipline by resorting to the external point of view provided by other disciplines. A way to do so is resorting to social sciences. Contraposing the empirical findings of the social sciences to the systematic reconstructions of legal reasoning prevents legal scholarship from cloaking the way in which law works, which results from taking at face value the internal point of view.

This set of oppositions (i.e. reductionism/anti-reductionism) correlates to opposite attitudes toward disciplinary boundaries: while anti-reductionists believe that something is lost by eroding disciplinary boundaries, reductionists believe that the conceptual frameworks that constitute disciplinary boundaries are obstacles for attaining knowledge. Likewise, as disciplinary boundaries are eroded, the internal point of view becomes less relevant for describing legal phenomena.

Furthermore, if one can only reason from within law's internal conceptual framework, its validity can never be questioned, beyond failures in the internal coherence of the system or mistakes in logical deduction (Gellner 1968). In this sense, the appeal of the external point of view is the promise of overcoming the categories of legal language, which (according to the critics)[3] muddle our thinking by diverting our attention from the real-world consequences of the allocation of resources to a formalized, technical language, impervious to what may come by a steadfast allegiance to age-old categories, which are at best an accidental historical vestige of past times. In other words, "[i]n comparison to traditional legal theory, Law and Economics is reductionist. Reductionism educates lawyers by scrapping unnecessary distinctions, which lawyers are prone to make" (Hylton 2019, p. 6).

These same features have been identified as the reasons why such an approach to legal phenomena should be rejected. Just like their anti-reductionist counterparts in philosophy of science, those who want to defend the autonomy of legal reasoning by stressing the necessity of the internal point of view argue that economic explanations disregard the noninstrumental normative considerations embedded in legal categories by reducing legal phenomena to their economic effects. For this reason, they reject economic explanations. They also argue that economic explanations disregard what legal institutions mean to the agents that engage with them (Zipursky 2006). The most extreme variety of this argument has been put forward by legal formalists (Grey 1999; Pildes 1999; F. Schauer 1988; Weinrib 2010). Insofar as legal formalists have made the most forceful defense of legal categories, it is worthwhile dwelling a little longer in the formalism debate in private law theory.

As noted, the debate between formalist and economic analysis of law in private law theory is a debate about the status of conceptual analysis within legal theory.

"The debate between the corrective justice theorists and the economists raises a more purely jurisprudential question about what legal theories must do to be acceptable. For while economists are boasting about their ability *to explain away* the plaintiff-driven nature of tort law in a

---

[3] See Gómez Pomar (2020).

reductive manner, corrective justice theorists are stating that *a theory that merely explains away structural features of the law in a reductive manner is for that very reason inadequate"* (Zipursky 2000, p. 458) [italics in the original].

As Zipursky lucidly notes, what for economists entails a relevant theoretical goal, for formalist legal theorists is the approach's main shortcoming. Formalists argue that economic analysis cannot accommodate the kind of reasoning that characterizes private law adjudication or its structural and procedural features (i.e. its bilateral structure of litigation) (Weinrib 2012). Likewise, with regards to the concept of rights, it has been argued that the bundle theory of rights (which underlies Neoclassical Law and Economics) cannot address the *in rem* character of property rights, that is the fact that one holds them against all other agents. Thus, it distorts central aspects of ownership, as it exists in Western legal systems (Penner 1995, 1997). The epitome of such a reductive perspective is Calabresi and Melamed's (1972) work on the economic analysis of property and liability rules in terms of entitlements. Critics argue that such an approach conflates the categories of property, contract and tort (Merrill and Smith 2001, pp. 379–383), and thus cannot account for the different normative values embedded in each of these institutions.

The economists' obvious response is to note that these normative values are not doing any work in legal reasoning, that is, they are of no help when trying to describe the content or predict the outcome of legal decisions. Consequently, if the formalists' anti-reductionist argument is to work, those additional normative considerations, which are supposedly irreducible, must be stated expressly, thus allowing the enquiry to continue. Otherwise, the anti-reductionist argument would boil down to assuming what it is supposed to demonstrate. This way, as legal theorists flesh out those (supposedly irreducible) features, economists can try to offer an account of them. For example, regarding the objection that economic analysis of law cannot accommodate the bilateral structure of private law adjudication, Kornhauser (2017) notes that even if efficiency-based accounts of private law don't consider the bilateral structure of private law as essential, they can account for its emergency and persistence.

The resulting trend is that, as economists put forward the hypothesis that legal reasoning can be reduced to economic reasoning or economic explanations, legal theorists can only try to refute the hypothesis by proposing a specific case of irreducibility. Economists can always answer the anti-reductionist argument, either on the grounds that (a) the additional normative considerations are intelligible in economic terms (i.e. are reducible) or (b) they are irrelevant to explain the subject matter, or (c) they are pathologic, exceptional or undesirable. In any case, economics' epistemic claim to explain legal phenomena remains untouched. Since the anti-reductionist strategy is inherently defensive, the best one can expect of it is to delay the encroachment of economics, but because of its very nature it can never stop it. Insofar as there is truth to the charges of economics' imperialism (Fine 2000, 2002; Lazear 2000; Mäki 2009; Nik-Khah and Van Horn 2012), it is a consequence of the strategy that legal theorists have taken to respond to the economists' challenge.

A positive aspect of this is that as the debate between anti-reductionist legal theorists and reductionist economists unfolds, new insights are obtained by the fleshing out of the normative considerations that are expressed in legal arrangements, while economists continue to apply their framework to each of these features. Unfortunately, this trend can only be maintained as long as legal theorists can continue their efforts. As economists manage to explain more aspects of law, the balance between law and economics grows increasingly unstable. The reason is simple: as the epistemic authority of economics grows, the epistemic authority of law dwindles.

Eventually, this change in the rationality aspect of disciplines affects the way in which the disciplines are practically organized, in terms of academic journals, curriculum reforms, postgraduate courses, research grants and so on (Landes and Posner 1993; Duxbury 2001). It is easy to see how these developments will eventually affect law at the institutional level: administrative officers, judges and legislators get educated under the new approach and the cumulative effect of their professional activity will be to make law resemble more and more the image of law they learned during their training. Most importantly, those who see it in their interest to support these developments will strive to do so (e.g. Teles 2008). For all the mentioned reasons, the character of legal academia matters and it can influence the development of legal systems. This is why legal education has been a contested domain from which to influence society and affect long-term legal change.

There is another way in which this pattern of disciplinary interaction reinforces the application of economics to the study of law. Mainstream economics tends to affirm the contingency of legal arrangements and the lack of any immanent rationality of law, while simultaneously portraying law as the result of a slow, piecemeal adaptation of the legal system to economic circumstances: a process of law working itself efficient. In this, mainstream economists agree with legal formalists insofar as the latter believe that legal categories are the result of a process of piecemeal evolution (Stein 2009). In this sense, mainstream Law and Economics supports the conservative bias of legal formalism by arguing that the goal of economics is to describe legal systems and not to prescribe how they ought to be (this strategy is captured by the distinction between positive and normative economics). The result is that legal arrangements have no immanent rationality, while at the same time any attempted reform would entail an illegitimate encroachment of real-world considerations into law, thus menacing the autonomy of legal rationality which purports to preserve the integrity of legal categories, which are the result of a slow process of evolution (see, for example, Hayek 1958).

For these reasons, the anti-reductionist strategy must be abandoned. Salvaging the autonomy of legal reasoning requires a balance of epistemic authority between legal theory and economics. This, in turn, requires increasing reflexivity in both disciplines. By reflexivity we mean here the activity of making explicit and questioning the underlying assumptions that guide reasoning within each discipline.

As defenders of economic analysis of law argue, it is the capacity of this approach to issue testable predictions that fosters the discipline's epistemic authority (Calabresi 2016). Here lies the key for the strategy that legal theorists should follow: they should move from the defensive anti-reductionist strategy to an offensive debunking strategy. Instead of just identifying (allegedly) irreducible features of law, which end up defining economics' expansionist agenda, legal theory should focus on undermining economics' claims to superior accuracy regarding predictions and causal explanation. This, of course, entails providing alternative methods for these tasks. In this sense, legal theory should go beyond conceptual analysis. Conceptual analysis, in this approach, would be necessary insofar as it helps to issue better predictions and explanations: it would be the beginning of the enquiry, not its end.

The predictions and explanations that current economic theory showcases constitute the minimum benchmark that legal theories should strive to attain.[4] Insofar as legal theory can adopt economics' epistemic goals

---

[4] It is important to notice that this is not a thesis about how judges should rule legal cases. This is a separate issue, which depends, first, on the place that consequentialist reasoning has within legal reasoning and, second, on whether economic analysis represents the best model of consequentialist reasoning. Neither of these questions is addressed by the argument

and not the other way around, the epistemic balance between both disciplines can be restored. In this sense, legal theory should uncover economics' blind spots and shortcomings. This will require legal theorists to probe other disciplines for the theoretical insights that will allow for improved empirical results, as well as better explanations. At the same time, social scientists who are concerned with issuing accurate predictions must adopt an approach that allows them to make sense of the legal categories that guide legal reasoning.

All of this requires a rehabilitation of Legal Realism. The general outline of such a project, based on Otto Neurath's non-foundationalist and non-reductive version of logical empiricism (Reisch 1994), is offered in the following section.

8.4   FOSTERING THE AUTONOMY OF LEGAL REASONING THROUGH LEGAL REALISM

As Jeremy Waldron (2000) has noted, legal realism bears the signs of logical empiricism's influence. This is no coincidence, since the anti-metaphysical stance of logical empiricism was common to both Scandinavian and American strands of legal realism, despite the other differences one might find between the two varieties (Alexander 2002; Bjarup 2005; Pihlajamäki 2004; Spaak 2017). For both varieties of realism, the integration between philosophy and social sciences was geared toward radical reformist impulses and a commitment with deepening democratic control of the legal institutions underlying the economic system. This goal was also shared by the left wing of the Vienna Circle (Sigmund 2017).

For Otto Neurath, one of the most interesting and prolific members of the Vienna Circle (Cat 2018), the integration of different disciplines was the ultimate aspiration of science. This required all the disciplines to develop their respective conceptual frameworks in such a way that the statements in one discipline could be connected and combined to the statements made in the others so that increasingly more accurate predictions could be made. Neurath's point was that each discipline was geared toward the production of theories, which in turn were developed to increase the predictive power of the disciplines. He reasoned that the fact

offered here. On consequence-based arguments in the context of legally bounded decision-making, see Cserne (2020).

that each discipline had developed different conceptual schemes hindered the integration of their results. Thus, even scholars within the same branch of science can be talking about the same phenomenon and it would not be clear whether they agree or not on its explanation (Neurath 1983b, pp. 172–173).

At the same time, issuing predictions about real-world phenomena requires the integration of knowledge of different branches of science. No real-life event is dependent exclusively on the laws of one definite discipline. Thus, predicting phenomena requires connecting or integrating the statements from different disciplines with each other (Neurath 1983a, p. 59).

At the same time, he argued that the different branches of science can be connected in multiple ways, with different goals in mind. Thus, the model for the totality of knowledge is a succession of overlapping "encyclopedias" or frameworks for the integration of scientific disciplines. This goal of organizing science was carried out in practice by Neurath within his project for an "Encyclopedia of Unified Science", inspired by the Encyclopédie of Diderot and D'Alembert. But unlike its predecessor, Neurath's "Encyclopedia of Unified Science" was assumed to be a provisional and historically bounded project, each iteration striving for more precision and systematization of all the available knowledge.

In this sense, Neurath was skeptical about disciplinary boundaries while at the same time renouncing to the idea that all the different disciplines could be reduced to a foundational metascience.

Likewise, for the rehabilitated version of legal realism proposed here, the sense of disciplinary unity behind this strategy for the division of intellectual labor is integration, as opposed to reduction (Fuller 2013). The point is not to reduce legal language to the language of economics; rather, the goal is to organize both disciplines to achieve the best possible picture of reality.

A good example of how such an approach could work can be taken from the recent scholarship regarding the fair use doctrine in copyright law. Professor Wendy Gordon proposed in a very influential article[5] that fair use should be available when the defendant can prove that high transaction costs preclude licensing and that the use serves an identifiable public benefit. The goal of Gordon's article was to illustrate how the courts

---

[5] The article was cited twice by the US Supreme Court in two major cases restricting fair use: *Sony v. Universal* (1984) and in the majority of *Harper & Row v. Nation Enterprises* (1985).

and Congress have employed fair use to permit uncompensated transfers that are socially desirable but not capable of effectuation through the market. The market approach will provide a guide both to ascertain where the public interest might lie in a given case and to identify those occasions on which a court may appropriately substitute its evaluation of the public interest for its usual refusal to second-guess the copyright owner (Gordon 1982, p. 1601).

In this sense, Gordon's article falls squarely within the reductionist program that has been commented on so far. In the following years, legal commentators questioned the usefulness of this "market-centered" approach to fair use, precisely on the grounds that it was not able to account for the considerations the courts actually used in adjudicating fair use cases—in particular, whether that use was transformative or not (Netanel 2011, pp. 734–736). This entailed that the transaction cost approach to fair use had to be complemented or corrected to better describe the judicial practice regarding the fair use doctrine. This task required making explicit normative considerations that were tacitly guiding legal reasoning. Of course, nothing guarantees that these seemingly extra-economic normative considerations cannot be reduced to the language of economics, but that requires crafting an economic model that can issue better predictions than the picture of law which includes noneconomic normative considerations.

Thus, the version of legal realism proposed here does not regard legal theory as merely a chapter of the social sciences, but grounds the former's autonomy in the fact that its conceptual scheme cannot be fully eliminated and, furthermore, it is necessary for accurate prediction.[6] Thus, by focusing on how legal science strives to make explicit tacit background assumptions underlying explicit law and issuing the best possible predictions regarding the working of law, this version of legal realism is concerned with how to integrate different "nodes" of the network of human knowledge. Inspired by Neurath's project, the possible interactions between the different disciplines which aim at explaining law can only advance insofar as their concepts can be translated across them, or a mutual language is developed by their respective practitioners.

---

[6] Of course, legal scholarship is not only about issuing better predictions; it also includes conceptual analysis, critique, justification, systematization, explanation and so forth. The point is rather that issuing better predictions is essential for law to keep its autonomy vis-à-vis the social sciences.

The goal is to achieve a language that is intelligible to practitioners of all the relevant disciplines and the normative aspiration is to acquire ever-increasing intelligibility across disciplines. Just like humanity, the task proposed here is strictly endless and ever-changing.

REFERENCES

Alexander, Gregory S. 2002. Comparing the Two Legal Realisms: American and Scandinavian. *The American Journal of Comparative Law* 50 (1): 131–174. https://doi.org/10.2307/840832.

Atria, Fernando. 2016. *La forma del derecho*. Madrid: Marcial Pons.

Bjarup, Jes. 2005. The Philosophy of Scandinavian Legal Realism. *Ratio Juris* 18 (1): 1–15. https://doi.org/10.1111/j.1467-9337.2005.00282.x.

Buchanan, James M., and Wm. Craig Stubblebine. 1962. Externality. *Economica* 29 (116): 371–384. https://doi.org/10.2307/2551386.

Calabresi, Guido. 2016. *The Future of Law and Economics: Essays in Reform and Recollection*. New Haven and London: Yale University Press.

Calabresi, Guido, and A. Douglas Melamed. 1972. Property Rules, Liability Rules, and Inalienability: One View of the Cathedral. *Harvard Law Review* 85 (6): 1089–1128. https://doi.org/10.2307/1340059.

Cat, Jordi. 2018. Otto Neurath. In *The Stanford Encyclopedia of Philosophy*, ed. Edward N. Zalta, Summer 2018. Metaphysics Research Lab, Stanford University. https://plato.stanford.edu/archives/sum2018/entries/neurath/

Commons, John R. 1924. *Legal Foundations of Capitalism*. New York: The Macmillan Company.

Cserne, Péter. 2020. Economic Approaches to Legal Reasoning: An Overview. In *Economics in Legal Reasoning*, ed. Péter Cserne and Fabrizio Esposito, 25–41. London: Palgrave Macmillan.

Duxbury, Neil. 2001. *Jurists and Judges: An Essay on Influence*. Oxford and Portland, OR: Hart.

Fine, Ben. 2000. Economics Imperialism and Intellectual Progress: The Present as History of Economic Thought? *History of Economics Review* 32 (1): 10–35. https://doi.org/10.1080/10370196.2000.11733338.

———. 2002. Economic Imperialism: A View from the Periphery. *Review of Radical Political Economics* 34: 187–201.

Fuller, Steve. 2013. Deviant Interdisciplinarity as Philosophical Practice: Prolegomena to Deep Intellectual History. *Synthese* 190 (11): 1899–1916.

Gellner, Ernest. 1968. The New Idealism—Cause and Meaning in the Social Sciences. In *Studies in Logic and the Foundations of Mathematics*, vol. 49, 377–432. Elsevier. https://doi.org/10.1016/S0049-237X(08)70510-X.

Gómez Pomar, Fernando. 2020. Characterizing Economic and Legal Approaches to the Regulation of Market Interactions. In *Economics in Legal Reasoning*, ed. Péter Cserne and Fabrizio Esposito, 63–79. London: Palgrave Macmillan.

Gordon, Wendy J. 1982. Fair Use as Market Failure: A Structural and Economic Analysis of the 'Betamax' Case and Its Predecessors. *Columbia Law Review* 82 (8): 1600–1657. https://doi.org/10.2307/1122296.

Grey, Thomas C. 1999. The New Formalism. *Stanford Public Law and Legal Theory Working Paper Series.* http://papers.ssrn.com/paper.taf?abstract_id=200732

Hayek, F.A. 1958. Freedom, Reason, and Tradition. *Ethics* 68 (4): 229–245.

Hylton, Keith. 2019. Law and Economics Versus Economic Analysis of Law. *European Journal of Law and Economics* 48: 77–88. https://doi.org/10.1007/s10657-018-9580-0.

Kornhauser, Lewis. 2017. The Economic Analysis of Law. In *The Stanford Encyclopedia of Philosophy*, ed. Edward N. Zalta, Fall 2017. Stanford University. https://plato.stanford.edu/archives/fall2017/entries/legal-econanalysis/

Landes, William M., and Richard A. Posner. 1993. The Influence of Economics on Law: A Quantitative Study. *The Journal of Law and Economics* 36 (1, Part 2): 385–424.

Lazear, Edward P. 2000. Economic Imperialism. *The Quarterly Journal of Economics* 115 (1): 99–146. https://doi.org/10.1162/003355300554683.

Leeson, Peter T. 2019. Do We Need Behavioral Economics to Explain Law? *European Journal of Law and Economics* 48 (1): 29–42. https://doi.org/10.1007/s10657-017-9573-4.

Mäki, Uskali. 2009. Economics Imperialism: Concept and Constraints. *Philosophy of the Social Sciences* 39 (3): 351–380. https://doi.org/10.1177/0048393108319023.

Mathis, Klaus, and Deborah Shannon. 2009. *Efficiency Instead of Justice?* Law and Philosophy Library, vol. 84. Dordrecht: Springer Netherlands. https://doi.org/10.1007/978-1-4020-9798-0.

Merrill, Thomas W., and Henry E. Smith. 2001. What Happened to Property in Law and Economics? *The Yale Law Journal* 111 (2): 357–398. https://doi.org/10.2307/797592.

Netanel, Neil. 2011. Making Sense of Fair Use. *Lewis & Clark Law Review* 15 (3): 715–772.

Neurath, Otto. 1983a. Sociology in the Framework of Physicalism. In *Philosophical Papers, 1913–1946*, ed. R. S. Cohen, Marie Neurath, and Carolyn R. Fawcett, 58–90. Vienna Circle Collection, vol. 16. Dordrecht, Holland and Boston, Hingham, MA: D. Riedel Pub. Co.

———. 1983b. Unified Science and Its Encyclopedia. In *Philosophical Papers, 1913–1946*, ed. R. S. Cohen, Marie Neurath, and Carolyn R. Fawcett, 172–182.

Vienna Circle Collection, vol. 16. Dordrecht, Holland and Boston, Hingham, MA: D. Riedel Pub. Co.

Nik-Khah, Edward, and Robert Van Horn. 2012. Inland Empire: Economics Imperialism as an Imperative of Chicago Neoliberalism. *Journal of Economic Methodology* 19 (3): 259–282. https://doi.org/10.108 0/1350178X.2012.714147.

Penner, James E. 1995. The Bundle of Rights Picture of Property. *UCLA Law Review* 43 (3): 711–820.

———. 1997. *The Idea of Property in Law*. Oxford, UK: Clarendon Press and Oxford University Press.

Pihlajamäki, Heikki. 2004. Against Metaphysics in Law: The Historical Background of American and Scandinavian Legal Realism Compared. *The American Journal of Comparative Law* 52 (2): 469–487. https://doi.org/10.2307/4144458.

Pildes, Richard H. 1999. Forms of Formalism. *The University of Chicago Law Review* 66 (3): 607–621. https://doi.org/10.2307/1600419.

Reisch, George A. 1994. Planning Science: Otto Neurath and the International Encyclopedia of Unified Science. *The British Journal for the History of Science* 27 (2): 153–175. https://doi.org/10.1017/S0007087400031873.

Schauer, Frederick. 1988. Formalism. *The Yale Law Journal* 97 (4): 509–548.

Schauer, Frederick F. 2009. *Thinking like a Lawyer: A New Introduction to Legal Reasoning*. Cambridge, MA: Harvard University Press.

Sigmund, Karl. 2017. *Exact Thinking in Demented Times: The Vienna Circle and the Epic Quest for the Foundations of Science*. New York: Basic Books.

Smith, Henry E. 2019. Complexity and the Cathedral: Making Law and Economics More Calabresian. *European Journal of Law and Economics* 48 (1): 43–63. https://doi.org/10.1007/s10657-018-9591-x.

Smith, Steven A. 2011. The Normativity of Private Law. *Oxford Journal of Legal Studies* 31 (2): 215–242. https://doi.org/10.1093/ojls/gqr002.

Spaak, Torben. 2017. Realism about the Nature of Law. *Ratio Juris* 30 (1): 75–104. https://doi.org/10.1111/raju.12073.

Stein, Peter. 2009. *Legal Evolution*. Cambridge: Cambridge University Press.

Teles, Steven Michael. 2008. *The Rise of the Conservative Legal Movement: The Battle for Control of the Law*. Princeton Studies in American Politics: Historical, International, and Comparative Perspectives. Princeton, NJ: Princeton University Press.

Waldron, Jeremy. 2000. 'Transcendental Nonsense' and System in the Law. *Columbia Law Review* 100 (1): 16–53. https://doi.org/10.2307/1123555.

Weinrib, Ernest J. 2010. Legal Formalism. In *A Companion to Philosophy of Law and Legal Theory*, ed. Dennis M. Patterson, 2nd ed., 327–339. Blackwell

Companions to Philosophy 8. Chichester, West Sussex and Malden, MA: Wiley-Blackwell.
———. 2012. *The Idea of Private Law*. Rev. ed. Oxford: Oxford University Press.
Zipursky, Benjamin C. 2000. Pragmatic Conceptualism. *Legal Theory* 6 (4): 457–485. https://doi.org/10.1017/S1352325200064053.
———. 2006. Legal Obligations and the Internal Aspect of Rules. *Fordham Law Review* 75 (3): 1229–1254.

CHAPTER 9

Reverse Engineering Legal Reasoning

Fabrizio Esposito

Abstract This chapter describes a novel and valuable approach to the relationship between economic analysis and the law called "reverse engineering legal reasoning". Social engineering conceives of the law as a means to social ends and of the economist as the technician studying to what extent laws are fit for purpose. Building on this idea, reverse engineering legal reasoning is a way to identify economic concepts that describe—are coherent with or fit—the content of legal reasoning. To do so, alternative economic hypotheses about the content of legal reasoning are formulated. On these grounds, the degree of coherence between economic concepts and legal reasoning can be made explicit. Reverse engineering legal reasoning extends the focus of positive economic analysis from the effects of the law to its content. It is useful for economists to suggest ways to increase the effectiveness of the legal system; to contribute to its functioning; as source of evidence to test economic assumptions; and to solve disagreements among economists, especially in relation to value choices.

F. Esposito (✉)
Université catholique de Louvain, Louvain-la-Neuve, Belgium
e-mail: fabrizio.esposito@uclouvain.be

© The Author(s) 2020
P. Cserne, F. Esposito (eds.), *Economics in Legal Reasoning*,
Palgrave Studies in Institutions, Economics and Law,
https://doi.org/10.1007/978-3-030-40168-9_9

Keywords Reverse engineering legal reasoning • Economics in legal reasoning • Efficiency hypothesis • Positive economics • Social engineer

9.1   INTRODUCTION

Legal reasoning is a rich and complex activity that has received too little attention from economists. Reverse engineering legal reasoning is a novel and valuable approach that can fill this gap by showing that a certain economic concept is more coherent with (describes or fits) legal reasoning than the alternatives. The main components of legal reasoning are the applicable norm, the reconstruction of fact, the arguments constituting their external justification, and the conclusion of the reasoning (Canale and Tuzet 2020). When legal reasoning is reverse-engineered, it becomes evidence that economists can use to foster the realism and practical significance of their research (see Sect. 9.3). More precisely, this is useful to identify the policy goal (the end) legal reasoning (the means) strives to achieve and to better understand how it tries to achieve its end.

Reverse engineering legal reasoning finds in Posner's efficiency hypothesis of the common law a precursor. Posner famously investigated "the hypothesis that common-law rules and institutions tend to promote economic efficiency" (1979, p. 285). Reverse engineering legal reasoning is also interested in the relationship between law and economic effects. However, the two approaches differ in important ways. First, reverse engineering legal reasoning compares the explanatory power of two (or more) hypotheses. For example, one could try to identify the image of consumers the law relies upon—how self-interested, (bounded) rational, informed, and so on they are. Likewise, one could try to identify the welfare standard applied in a certain branch of the law. The difference with Posner's approach is marked because he tried to make sense of the common law from a particular economic perspective—the promotion of economic efficiency, understood as wealth maximization—instead of comparing if it made more sense under one perspective or another. Notably, as reverse engineering is a comparative analysis of a limited set of hypotheses, it cannot be ruled out that an unconsidered hypothesis would have an even superior explanatory power.

Second, Posner's efficiency hypothesis was about the efficiency of the incentive structure actually created by the law. It was about the law's effects in relation to an economic goal, external to legal reasoning

(Esposito and Tuzet 2019, pp. 138–140). This is another significant difference because when one reverse-engineers legal reasoning the focus is on the content of legal reasoning, not on its effects. For example, when one reverse-engineers, what matters is the degree of rationality attributed to consumers by judges—which may be different from both their actual degree of rationality and the degree normally assumed among economists. In other words, Posner's efficiency hypothesis belongs to the economics of legal reasoning, while reverse engineering legal reasoning is about the economics (currently) in legal reasoning (on the distinction, see Cserne 2020).

The chapter is structured as follows. Section 9.2 shows the economic roots of the idea of reverse engineering legal reasoning. These roots lie in the division between positive and normative economics and in the paradigm of the economist as a social engineer. Section 9.3 elaborates on the scope of reverse engineering legal reasoning. Reverse engineering shifts the focus from the effects of the law to its content. This feature is particularly attractive in relation to value choices, where reverse engineering the law means to pay paramount attention to the intended consequences of the law. At this point, the effects of the law regain relevance. If, once reverse-engineered, the law is found 'defective'—in particular, ineffective—proposals to reengineer it are welcome. Section 9.4 describes the main methodological features of reverse engineering legal reasoning. First, one needs to identify alternative economic concepts implying differences in legal reasoning. Second, one has to compare the degree of coherence between the economic concepts and the observed reasoning. Third, when there is more than one datapoint, criteria for aggregating the results are necessary. Section 9.5 recaps and concludes.

9.2 The Roots: Positive Economic Analysis and Social Engineering

To put the idea of reverse engineering legal reasoning into context, two concepts are of great help. The first is the distinction between positive and normative economic analysis. The second is the idea of the economist as a social engineer.

The distinction between positive and normative discourse is one of the basic concepts one learns early on in both economics and legal studies. In a first approximation, positive discourse is about how the world is or how we see it, whereas normative discourse is about how the world ought to be or how we want it to be. For example, "I think tomorrow will be a rainy day" is an instance of positive discourse. I might desire tomorrow to be a sunny day while believing that it will rain.

Positive economic analysis, as an instance of positive discourse in general, aims at telling us something about how the world is. Of course, there is some degree of variety within the questions that can be answered with positive analysis. One can try to explain economic phenomena—which causal mechanisms are at play in this context? One can try to estimate phenomena—what is the value of such-and-such indicator? One can try to predict outcomes—what will be the effect of such-and-such action? Importantly, for our purposes, one can also try to find the means to reach given ends—how can this goal be reached? This last point is particularly important. In describing positive analysis, emphasis is normally placed on the first three tasks: explanation, estimation, and prediction (Friedman 1953). But the contribution of positive analysis to action-guiding shall not be forgotten. As Posner puts it, our 'positive' interest "in the economic and legal systems is practical; it is an interest in making these things work better"; ultimately, we are interested in "learning how to do things" (2015, p. 4).

Take, for example, the much celebrated (and contested) analysis of Kaplow and Shavell (1994) which argues that distributive concerns are better addressed by the tax system rather than by private law. The authors do not claim that distributive concerns do not matter at all. That would be a normative claim. They simply argue that (under robust conditions—at least, this is their view) any level of redistribution of income can be achieved with less waste of resources using the tax system instead of private law. This is a claim about the superior productive efficiency of one means (the tax system) over another (private law). It is interesting to note that the necessity test used in the framework of proportionality reasoning can also be understood in the same way (see Esposito 2018a).

The paradigm of the economist as a social engineer gives prominence to analyses like the one by Kaplow and Shavell. Social engineering, in the neutral sense of the expression, aims at informing policy choices in light of instrumental or causal considerations connecting given ends to the means that allow achieving those ends (Davidson 2010). Social engineering does not even have to identify which means would be best, all things considered. Unless the end is fully specified, different means will generate different degrees of effectiveness and costs, so that selecting the best means to pursue a given end is a choice that can very easily trespass the line between positive and normative analysis. In sum, the image of economic analysis as social engineering presents the economist as the technician studying to what extent laws are fit for purpose.

Reverse engineering legal reasoning, from an economic perspective, is an instance of positive discourse. More precisely, as its name suggests, it is an extension of the social engineer paradigm. Both study the relation between possible means and social ends. However, the difference lies in what is to be found. The social engineer knows the end to be reached and focuses on finding the adequate means. In the case of reverse engineering, one can do two things: one may either look at legal reasoning (the means) to identify the policy goal it strives to achieve (the end) or one may look at legal reasoning to better understand how it is trying to achieve its end.

9.3   Why: Among Other Things, to Reverse-engineer and Then Reengineer

We have seen that reverse engineering legal reasoning is an idea that belongs to the realm of positive economic analysis and is an organic development of the social engineer paradigm. Reverse engineering legal reasoning is intended to infer the ends by looking at how the means are used, and to better understand the means themselves.

Why would one want to do reverse engineering legal reasoning? The subtitle of this section captures the main reason: Reverse-engineer, then reengineer. Reverse engineering legal reasoning is a preliminary step to improve the design of the legal system on its own terms; in other words, to make the law more effective in the pursuit of its intended goals. Consistently with the social engineer paradigm, the task at the reengineering stage will not be offering a normative critique of policy goals. The task will be offering better tools to achieve the given ends. Obviously, it might be the case that, once reverse-engineered, the law might attract normative critiques aimed at changing the policy goals it pursues. But, as noted in Sect. 9.2, in so doing we would be outside the realm of positive analysis.

Moreover, reverse engineering legal reasoning is arguably a preliminary step to social engineering it. The social engineer paradigm entails a division of labor according to which economists (the social engineers) have to study the relation between given ends and possible means. Accordingly, economists need to know what the law intends to do in order to assess if it could do it better. To put it differently, social engineering is about the economic analysis of the intended consequences of the law. Reverse engineering legal reasoning allows a better understanding of what the law is trying to achieve and how it tries to achieve it.

A related reason applies specifically, but importantly, to disagreements among economists on value choices. According to the social engineer paradigm, economists should be reluctant to make value choices themselves in their analysis. Making value choices belongs to the realm of normative discourse, and the social engineer tries to stay away from it. Accordingly, it becomes particularly difficult to take a principled stance in case of disagreement about the normative standard to use. Yet, disagreements of this sort are quite common even within the economic analysis of law, although they do not attract much academic attention.

Traditionally, the economic analysis of law has built on the idea that the general goal of the legal system is the maximization of total welfare, while distributive goals are pursued by specialized branches of the legal system, mainly taxes and subsidies (Kaplow and Shavell 2002; Devlin 2015). One limit of this general account is that several branches of the legal system are described in economic terms as having different goals by specialized scholars. Contract law, especially in case of commercial contracts, focuses on the joint surplus of the parties (Scott and Schwartz 2003); corporate governance focuses on shareholder value (Hansmann and Kraakman 2001); competition law and consumer law focus on consumer welfare (Esposito 2018b, pp. 189–254). To be sure, in each and every of these (and other) cases, one can find many examples of analysis adopting a total welfare standard. One reason why there is so much variety is that there are two types of economists of law: field specialists and multi-field scholars (Schwartz 2001). What matters here is that these disagreements exist.

Reverse engineering legal reasoning offers a possible way to solve these disagreements. The law is a normatively committed institution—it claims the authority to direct, organize, and govern the behavior of its subjects (Raz 1979). Accordingly, if one were to find that a specific branch of the law is significantly more coherent with one welfare standard instead of the other, this finding would be a reason to solve the disagreement in favor of the more coherent standard (Esposito and Tuzet 2019, pp. 135–136). Of course, the law's claim to authority can be challenged on moral grounds. But the same could be said about the choice of this or that welfare standard. A welfare standard is, after all, a value choice. Those unwilling to engage in moral argumentation—for example, social engineers—can defer to the legal system the selection of the welfare standard and focus on the best means to maximize it.

Third, reverse engineering legal reasoning has heuristic value for economists (Calabresi 2016; Esposito 2019). If economic theory typically operates with a certain assumption, finding out that legal practice operates on a different one might be a reason to reconsider the soundness of the economic assumption. Of course, contrary to the case of value choices, legal practice does not claim any epistemic authority against economic theory. Nevertheless, it might be that legal reasoning had good reasons to incorporate assumptions that are different from those incorporated in economic theory, but economists have difficulty in grasping these reasons from outside legal practice. The level of rationality of consumers is a good example of this. Building on rational choice theory, the unconscionability doctrine has received lots of critiques in the past (Epstein 1975; Farber 2000). When invoking such a protection, consumers were seen as trying to walk away from agreements that made them better off *ex ante*. Once the rationality assumption is relaxed, the unconscionability doctrine makes much more sense from an economic perspective (Korobkin 2003; Esposito 2017, pp. 208–210). Had the unconscionability doctrine been taken as an anomaly for rational choice theory, behavioral studies might have developed more quickly.

Fourth, reverse engineering legal reasoning is useful already for those who simply want to participate in the functioning of the legal system, without any ambition to change it, like forensic economists (see Broulík 2020). As Giocoli (2020) notes, the uncertainty in relation to the relevance of economic models with regard to particular issues disproportionately exposes economics expert testimonies to admissibility challenges under US law in antitrust litigation. Enhancing coherence with legal reasoning makes economic expert testimonies more relevant and, therefore, more resistant to admissibility challenges.

Finally, reverse engineering legal reasoning is also of use to those who do not accept the social engineer paradigm. Economists give more effective policy advice if they move from a sound understanding of the content of the relevant legal reasoning (Cserne 2020; Figueroa Zimmermann 2020). The more legally informed economic analysis is, the more persuasive it will be within the legal community. If, for example, competition policy assumes a consumer welfare standard, it is clear that an economic analysis building on such a standard will be more relevant in a competition law case than an analysis using a total welfare standard. It is of course still possible to criticize the soundness of such a standard—but doing so requires knowing that it is the standard that best fits with the law as it currently is, something reverse engineering legal reasoning helps ascertain.

9.4   How: Economic Hypotheses and Fitness Check

To reverse-engineer legal reasoning, one needs two things. First, one needs competing economic hypotheses[1] to generate competing explanations of the content of legal reasoning. Second, one needs a method to analyze legal reasoning to establish which economic hypothesis fits better with legal reasoning. The two are connected, but can be kept relatively separate for explanatory purposes.

9.4.1   Building the Competing Economic Hypotheses

The competing economic hypotheses are built by reference to economic literature broadly understood. Arguably, any hypothesis with consequences for economic research—however unpopular in current economic research—should be taken into consideration. As mentioned in Sect. 9.1, it is essential to have at least two competing hypotheses in order to compare their explanatory power. Moreover, the hypotheses may have to do with normative or empirical variables; for example, the welfare standard to be used is a normative variable, whereas the level of transaction costs is an empirical one.

The task is to identify differences in the arguments built on one concept or the other. Consider the mainstream framework for the analysis of the choice between property and liability rules (injunctions vs damages) and the choice of remedies in private law matters. In the simple setting that is uninterested in distributive issues, if transaction costs are low (in comparison to adjudication costs), a property rule is to be preferred; if transaction costs are high (in comparison to adjudication costs), a liability rule is to be preferred (Cooter and Ulen 2012, pp. 94–102; Komesar 1994, pp. 14–28). The intuition behind this difference is that if transaction costs are low, the parties will reach the efficient solution—the solution that maximizes total welfare—at a lower cost than courts; if these costs are high, the opposite

---

[1] Given its intended audience, this chapter focuses on the use of reverse engineering in relation to economics, but this approach can be used to test hypotheses coming from any discipline.

is true. This economic lesson about efficient remedies can be easily turned into two competing economic hypotheses, to be tested analyzing legal reasoning.

These two competing economic hypotheses can be tested in a rather simple way. When courts apply a property rule, they consider transaction cost to be low (in comparison to adjudication costs). When courts apply a liability rule, they consider transaction costs to be high (in comparison to adjudication costs). This is, of course, true, under the twofold assumption that courts care only about total welfare maximization and will make their decision on the basis of the level of transaction costs (in comparison to adjudication costs). Additionally, if courts justify their decision by referring to the level of transaction costs, the inference becomes even more convincing.

The example of transaction costs is very simple, but its simplicity allows us to make some important observations. In the example, the idea that the policy goal is total welfare maximization is another economic assumption—one about value choices—that needs testing. It could be that other policy goals would lead to overlapping results with total welfare maximization; in other words, the different policy goals would diverge in justification but converge in outcomes. As long as this is the case, the policy goal is not relevant to reverse-engineer the institutional belief in relation to the level of transaction costs. However, it could also be that the policy goal is a complex one. For example, the seminal contribution by Calabresi and Melamed (1972) on the choice between property and liability rules considered also distributive concerns (and inalienability rules). This difficulty illustrates a simple general point about reverse engineering legal reasoning. Value and institutional choices are intertwined in legal reasoning, and finding ways to analyze one type of choice without the interference of the other is a significant challenge in terms of research design.

Second, it is easier to study value choices than institutional choices. This is the case because, as noted in Sect. 9.1, the economic analysis of law often adopts a total welfare standard as a general matter, but then different welfare standards are adopted locally. Likewise, the views of scholars operating outside the economic tradition might help in generating competing economic assumptions. All these divergent perspectives are likely to harbor valuable insight for building competing economic hypotheses. For example, if consumer law is about the maximization of consumer welfare, the welfare standard incorporates the distribution of welfare between the contractual parties. Accordingly, it is efficient for damages in case of breach of contract by the trader to have a compensatory function in favor of consumers. This idea is in contrast with the familiar economic view that the choice between expectation and reliance damages is indeterminate as long as they deter breaches that reduce total welfare (Kaplow and Shavell 2002, p. 181; Katz 2015, p. 185). At the same time, the idea that expectation damages are normally more efficient follows rather simply from a consumer welfare standard.

Finally, when ones tests competing economic hypotheses, it is important to remember that our evidence is the reasoning. For example, a perfectly competitive market maximizes both total and consumer welfare (Esposito 2018b, pp. 84–86)—that is the competitive single-market equilibrium is a first-best outcome under both welfare standards. However, when explaining or justifying the desirability of perfectly competitive markets, one will reason differently from a total or a consumer welfare standard. Ultimately, one will offer a justification to the view that a perfectly competitive market is desirable because it maximizes total welfare; or one will offer a justification to the view that a perfectly competitive market is desirable because it maximizes consumer welfare. Accordingly, convergence in outcomes does not rule out divergence in reasoning and it is this divergence that matters when one reverse-engineers legal reasoning.

To sum up, to build competing economic hypotheses, one has to identify where alternative economic concepts imply different reasoning. Value and institutional choices are intertwined, but separate, and value choices are relatively simpler to reverse-engineer. Finally, it is important to remember that the conflict we are interested in is about differences in reasoning, not difference in outcomes.

9.4.2   Fitness Check

The fitness check looks at legal reasoning to compare the degree of coherence or fit the competing economic hypotheses with legal reasoning.[2] To do so, one needs a method of analysis, a measurement system, and, in case of more than one datapoint, an aggregation method.

---

[2] Esposito (2019) argues that this type of fitness check is a necessary distinctive feature of what Calabresi (2016) calls "Law and Economics" vis-à-vis the "Economic Analysis of Law". This is a point that has passed essentially unnoticed in the literature elaborating on Calabresi's distinction. See, for example, Bix (2019), Hylton (2019), and Marciano and Ramello (2019).

The method of analysis consists essentially in constructing a reasoning meshing one economic hypothesis together with the actual legal reasoning. This activity is performed for all the economic hypotheses under consideration. Reconsider the example about the relationship between the level of transaction costs and the alternative between property and liability rules. Assume that in a nuisance case involving only two neighbors, the defendant is ordered to cease the activity generating the nuisance. The hypothesis stating that transaction costs are low explains this decision straightforwardly: as it is efficient to apply a property rule when transaction costs are low and the judge has applied a property rule, the transaction costs must have been low according to the judge; indeed, the small number of parties involved suggests the transaction costs were low. The hypothesis stating that transaction costs are high fails to explain this decision because, according to it, had transaction costs been high, the judge would have applied a liability rule.

In a case as simple as this, to adjudicate between the competing economic hypotheses, one does not really need a measurement system because one hypothesis matches perfectly with the evidence while the other does not match at all. In other words, the first hypothesis is coherent with the evidence while the second one clearly is not. However, it is rarely the case that results are so clear in reality. Judges normally avoid articulating the reasons justifying their decisions in full (Sunstein 2018). Accordingly, it is useful to introduce at least a measurement system that allows distinguishing between good, acceptable, and inacceptable explanations (Esposito 2018b, pp. 181–184). In the previous example, we had two extreme examples of good and inacceptable explanations. One explanation fit perfectly with the evidence, while the other was not even formulated because it would have been impossible to connect the hypothesis and the evidence in a coherent manner.

When legal reasoning is too shallow, however, it is possible for a hypothesis to offer a merely acceptable explanation. An explanation is merely acceptable when it fills to a large extent the silence in the legal reasoning with the content of the hypothesis itself. Imagine, for example, that in the nuisance case under consideration, the judge awards damages for the past and imposes an injunction for the future. Does this mean that transaction costs were high or low according to the judge? One could argue that transaction costs were low, because the most important decision—what to do for the future—remains in the hands of the parties. One could also argue that transaction costs were high, because the most controversial decision—what to do for the past—was made by the judge. Both hypotheses make sense and do not contradict the information available about the decision. However, they both inject an important information in the reasoning of the court that was not there: namely what the most conflictual aspect of the interaction is—deciding about the past or about the future. We do not have information on this point, which is, however, essential for both explanations under consideration. Notably, it is often the case that competing explanations have a symmetrical relationship with the evidence, so that if one is good, the other is unacceptable or vice versa, or both tend to be acceptable. This symmetry comes from the fact that when reasoning is shallow, ample room is left for ingenuity to step in and fill the silence in the reasoning. However, this is not necessarily the case. In fact, if a piece of information is irrelevant to one explanation but important (positively or negatively) for the other, then it might well happen that one hypothesis delivers an acceptable explanation, while the other offers a polar explanation.

In the discussion about nuisance, the hypotheses about the level of transaction costs were essentially tested on a very limited portion of legal reasoning, namely the rules that are applied. But, as noted, legal reasoning is not made only of rules (normative premises), but also of facts (factual premises), the justification of both, and the application of the rule to the facts (see Canale and Tuzet 2020). By extending the analysis to these other elements of the legal reasoning, one can enrich the quality of the explanatory analysis. To some extent, this is what happened when the number of parties involved was used to corroborate the observation that transaction costs were low; but many other elements might be relevant (Cooter and Ulen 2012, pp. 88–91). Take the famous *Boomer v Atlantic Cement Company* case,[3] at the heart of the discussion on property and liability rules. The court awarded damages in a situation where the law had granted an injunction so far. The reason for this unusual decision is to be found in the disproportion between the damage suffered by the plaintiffs, quantified in 185.000 USD of 1970, and the shutting down of a cement factory involving an investment of 45 million USD of 1970 and employing 300 people. Writing for the majority, Judge Bergan noted that "to follow the rule literally in these cases would be to close down the plant at once. This court is fully agreed to avoid that immediately drastic remedy; the difference in view is how best to avoid it." The dissenting judge

[3] 26 N.Y.2d 219, 309 N.Y.S.2d 312 (N.Y. 1970).

supported issuing an injunction if no solution was found after 18 months of negotiations. The solution of the controversy indeed revolves around the level of transaction costs (Komesar 1994, pp. 14–26). In a nutshell, contrary to the dissenting judge, the majority did not believe that a solution to reduce the level of pollution could be found in the near future. Accordingly, the competing economic hypotheses imply that the decision can be reverse-engineered to conclude that the majority considered transaction costs higher than the adjudication costs.

The larger the dataset, the more comprehensive and therefore telling are the results. As judges do not articulate in full the reasons justifying their decisions, when one analyzes a handful of cases, it is possible for all the competing hypotheses to offer acceptable explanations (e.g., Esposito and Tuzet 2020). It goes without saying that the dataset should be built in order to avoid cherry-picking. The gold standard would be to analyze the entire population of cases related to a certain issue. When this is unfeasible, it is necessary to justify both the scope limitation and the specific cases selected within that scope. In relation to the scope, it is advisable to move from the most relevant context, and then extend the scope as far as feasible. In relation to case selection, it is advisable to defer to an external authority, like the cases discussed in several academic publications on the matter.

Having more than one datapoint requires a rule for aggregating the results. It is appropriate to give significantly more weight to polar results—that is, good and inacceptable explanations—*vis-à-vis* merely acceptable ones. One way to do this is aggregating explanations according to a polar attraction rule, namely polar results attract (or absorb) acceptable explanations. Thus, a good explanation attracts an acceptable one; likewise, an inacceptable explanation attracts an acceptable one. The reason for this aggregation rule is that clearer explanations are better explanations. Polar explanations establish a stronger connection with legal reasoning; they dig deep enough to conclude that the economic and legal concepts under consideration are either coherent or incoherent. If a hypothesis offers opposite polar explanations, the implication is that the hypothesis offers only an acceptable explanation. This is indeed an interesting result, as it may suggest that the dataset was not properly selected, or it may signal that there is an incoherence between the decisions included in the dataset—something of immediate consequence in legal practice.

9.5   CONCLUSION

Reverse engineering legal reasoning is a novel approach to the relationship between economic analysis and law that focuses on the study of the coherence or fit between economic concepts and legal reasoning. It focuses, in other words, on establishing which economic concept better describes the content of legal reasoning. Reverse engineering legal reasoning belongs to the positive branch of economics and is closely connected to the social engineer paradigm, according to which economists study the relation between alternative means and given ends.

For economists, reverse engineering legal reasoning is particularly useful to suggest ways to increase the effectiveness of the legal system; to contribute to its functioning; as a source of evidence to test economic assumptions; to solve disagreements among economists, especially in relation to value choices.

Contrary to traditional economic analysis, the study of the effects of the law remains in the background, as the focus is on the concepts used in legal reasoning. Considerations about the effects of the law matter when economic analysis shows that the actual (predicted or observed) effects of the law are different from the intended ones. Yet, to find out what the intended effects are, one can reverse-engineer legal reasoning. Reverse engineering legal reasoning is thus complementary to traditional economic analysis of law.

REFERENCES

Bix, Brian H. 2019. Law and Economics and the Role of Explanation: A Comment of Guido Calabresi, The Future of Law and Economics. *European Journal of Law and Economics* 48: 113–123.

Broulík, Jan. 2020. What is Forensic Economics? In *Economics in Legal Reasoning*, ed. Péter Cserne and Fabrizio Esposito, 83–99. London: Palgrave Macmillan.

Calabresi, Guido. 2016. *The Future of Law and Economics: Essays in Reform and Recollection*. New Haven: Yale University Press.

Calabresi, Guido, and Douglas A. Melamed. 1972. Property Rules, Liability Rules, and Inalienability: One View of the Cathedral. *Harvard Law Review* 85: 1089–1128.

Canale, Damiano, and Giovanni Tuzet. 2020. What is Legal Reasoning About: A Jurisprudential Perspective. In *Economics in Legal Reasoning*, ed. Péter Cserne and Fabrizio Esposito, 9–24. London: Palgrave Macmillan.

Cooter, Robert D., and Thomas H. Ulen. 2012. *Law & Economics*. 6th ed. New York: Addison-Wesley.

Cserne, Péter. 2020. Economic Approaches to Legal Reasoning: An Overview. In *Economics in Legal Reasoning*, ed. Péter Cserne and Fabrizio Esposito, 25–41. London: Palgrave Macmillan.

Davidson Sinclair. 2010. *Economists as Social Engineers*. Melbourne: Institute of Public Affairs.

Devlin, Alan. 2015. *Fundamental Principles of Law and Economics*. London: Routledge.

Epstein, Richard A. 1975. Unconscionability: A Critical Reappraisal. *The Journal of Law and Economics* 18: 293–315.

Esposito, Fabrizio. 2017. A Dismal Reality: Behavioural Analysis and Consumer Policy. *Journal of Consumer Policy* 40: 193–216.

———. 2018a. Economic Concepts in the Analysis of Proportionality Reasoning between Similarity and Identity. *Analisi e Diritto* 1/2018: 185–210.

———. 2018b. *Law and Economics United in Diversity: Minimalism, Fairness, and Consumer Welfare in EU Antitrust and Consumer Law*. PhD diss., European University Institute.

———. 2019. On the Fitness between Law and Economics—Or Sunstein between Posner and Calabresi. *Global Jurist* 19. https://doi.org/10.1515/gj-2018-0054.

Esposito, Fabrizio, and Giovanni Tuzet. 2019. Economic Consequences as Legal Values: An Inferentialist Approach. In *Law and Economics as Interdisciplinary Exchange*, ed. Péter Cserne and Magdalena Malecka, 123–157. Abingdon: Routledge.

———. 2020. Economic Consequences for Lawyers: Beyond the Jurisprudential Preface. *Journal of Argumentation* (forthcoming).

Farber, Daniel A. 2000. Economic Efficiency and the Ex Ante Perspective. In *The Jurisprudential Foundations of Corporate and Commercial Law*, ed. Jody M. Kraus and Steven D. Walt, 121–137. Cambridge: Cambridge University Press.

Figueroa Zimmermann, Felipe. 2020. Fostering the autonomy of legal reasoning through Legal Realism. In *Economics in Legal Reasoning*, ed. Péter Cserne and Fabrizio Esposito, 121–137. London: Palgrave Macmillan.

Friedman, Milton. 1953. The Methodology of Positive Economics. In *Essays in Positive Economics*. Chicago: The University of Chicago Press.

Giocoli, Nicola. 2020. Why US Judges Reject Economic Experts? In *Economics in Legal Reasoning*, ed. Péter Cserne and Fabrizio Esposito, 101–117. London: Palgrave Macmillan.

Hansmann, Henry, and Reinier H. Kraakman. 2001. The End of History For Corporate Law. *Georgetown Law Journal* 89: 439–468.

Hylton, Keith N. 2019. Law and Economics Versus Economic Analysis of Law. *European Journal of Law and Economics* 48: 77–88.

Kaplow, Louis, and Steven Shavell. 1994. Why the Legal System is Less Efficient than the Income Tax in Redistributing Income. *Journal of Legal Studies* 23 (2): 667–681.

———. 2002. *Fairness versus Welfare*. Boston: Harvard University Press.

Katz, Avery W. 2015. Economic Foundations of Contract Law. In *Philosophical Foundations of Contract Law*, ed. Gregory Klass, George Letsas, and Price Saprai, 171–192. New York: Oxford University Press.

Komesar, Neil. 1994. *Imperfect Alternatives*. Chicago: The University of Chicago Press.

Korobkin, Russel. 2003. Bounded Rationality, Standard Form Contracts, and Unconscionability. *The University of Chicago Law Review* 70: 1203–1295.

Marciano, Alain, and Giovanni Battista Ramello. 2019. Law, Economics and Calabresi on the Future of Law and Economics. *European Journal of Law and Economics* 48: 65–76.

Posner, Richard A. 1979. Some Uses and Abuses of Economics in Law. *The University of Chicago Law Review* 46: 281–306.

———. 2015. Norms and Values in the Economic Approach to Law. In *Law and Economics: Philosophical Issues and Fundamental Questions*, ed. Aristides Hatzis and Nicholas Mercuro, 1–15. Abingdon: Routledge.

Raz, Joseph H. 1979. *The Authority of Law*. Oxford: Oxford University Press.

Schwartz, Alan. 2001. Two Culture Problems in Law and Economics. *University of Illinois Law Review* 5/2011: 1531–1550.

Scott, Robert E., and Alan Schwartz. 2003. Contract Theory and the Limits of Contract Law. *The Yale Law Journal* 113: 541–619.

Sunstein, Cass R. 2018. *Legal Reasoning and Political Conflict*. 2nd ed. New York: Oxford University Press.

Index[1]

---

[1] Note: Page numbers followed by 'n' refer to notes.

9 783030 401672